I0842792

Jewish Defense League:
The Early Years

A Study in Ethnic Conflict and Political Violence

by Steven C. Siesser

First paperback edition, December 2021

The author is not responsible for websites (or their content) that are not owned by the author.

ISBN 978-1-716-45864-4

Acknowledgement is made to Getty Images for permission to print images appearing on pages 34, 45 and 66.

10 9 8 7 6 5 4 3 2 1

Printed in the United States of America

It happened in those days that Moses grew up and went out to his brethren and observed their burdens; and he saw an Egyptian man striking a Hebrew man, of his brethren. He turned this way and that and saw that there was no man, so he struck down the Egyptian and hid him in the sand.
(Exodus, 2:11-12)

"He didn't look at this act and say, 'Let's form a committee to study the root causes of anti-Semitism'. Instead, he smote the Egyptian."
(Rabbi Meir Kahane)

Table of Contents

Preface

Anti-Semitic slogans appear on buildings throughout the city. Cemeteries are desecrated. Jews in New York are harassed and beaten on the streets of Brooklyn, attacked with machetes in their home in Monsey and gunned down in their shop in Jersey City, NJ. The number of anti-Semitic hate crimes being committed throughout the region is alarmingly up and the Anti-Defamation League organizes demonstrations to show unity in support of terrorized Jews.

The mayor of New York pledges his support and action, but delivers neither and instead slashes funding for nonprofits fighting bigotry. The Jewish Establishment and ultra-orthodox groups are publicly undercutting and clashing with each other in the media. Jews are talking about taking self-defense classes and buying guns. A group of activists come together to form the Community Security Service which trains ordinary congregants to patrol their synagogues and protect against attackers.

The year is 2020, but it might as well be 1968.

In this book, I examine the relationship between social conflict, political violence and the strategic role it plays in determining political outcomes. We will learn how a small, committed group of activists come together, forming the Jewish Defense League, to fill a political void. In the face of steep opposition from the Jewish Establishment, I will trace how the JDL, in a few short years, left its mark and achieved political gains using methods that were denounced at the time but whose strategies have served as a model for those activists who came after them.

Thanks goes to my editorial circle consisting of Jerry Katzoff, Ken Horowitz and Gary Fellman. Their insight and suggestions have proven invaluable and I greatly appreciate the time and effort they devoted to this project.

I would like to acknowledge and thank Martin A. Schain, Professor of Politics, Emeritus, at New York University. He has taught in France, and lectured throughout Europe and is the author of many books. Professor Schain is the founder and former director of the Center for European Studies at New York University, and former chair of the European Union Studies Association. He provided me guidance and motivation as I prepared the original manuscript in 1972 that ultimately resulted in the publication of this book.

Thanks also goes to my son, Ronald A. Siesser, who has heard me talk about this manuscript for years. Ron served as my editor, making significant contributions to the organization of the book and providing his masterful expertise in detailed editing. Mostly, I thank him for helping me fulfill my long-talked about dream by taking on the task of all the production aspects to publish this book. Finally, it's done.

Steven C. Siesser

October 2021

Theories of Social Change

The use of violence to extract political gains is not a new phenomenon in American society as some of our leaders would have us believe. Our history is coated with incidents of domestic political violence: The treatment of Native Americans, the enslavement of blacks, the Whiskey Rebellion, the Civil War draft riot in New York, the post-civil war treatment of blacks, the Pullman Strikes, the civil rights movement, and the on-campus student rebellion resulting from the war in Vietnam. More recent examples include the activities of white supremacists, radical environmentalists and the Occupy Wall Street movement, just to cite a few.

The intensification of group conflict and use of violent strategies for the achievement of social and political goals has led some of our more prominent leaders to declare America to be a "sick" society. Moreover, following the assassinations of the Reverend Martin Luther King and Senator Robert F. Kennedy, a commission was formed by President Lyndon B. Johnson in June 1968 to investigate violence and crime in the United States with the hope that such a move would satisfy the loudest voices and cause the problem to vanish by itself. Yet, the proliferation of group conflict and the application of violent strategies as a political tool has become more common than ever before.

Extensive research has been conducted on conflict and violence. These studies have delved into such areas as: the origin of conflict and violence, the history of violence, the definition and classification of different kinds and degrees of conflict and violence, condemnation and justification for the use of violence, resolving conflicts and violence, and even a functionalist approach to social conflict as useful in the "maintenance, adjustment or adaptation of social relationships and social structures."[1]

Most of these studies share one basic premise: Conflict and violence as political tools are viewed as abnormal, deviant behavior in American society by those who abhor its use and even by some who resort to its use. In the latter case, a rationale is usually employed appealing to the rest of the society for understanding of the group's particular plight. It is because of this basic premise that these various studies have fallen short in their analyses.

The use of violence is an historical fact and a function of human nature, not extraordinary or anomalous. Violence in all its forms is an intrinsic element of political behavior. Most sociologists and political scientists have declined to acknowledge this fact. It would be paradoxical to their basic premise if they were to adopt the principle that political violence is a natural form of political behavior. That it is not viewed as such is also a "consequence of selective historical recollection."[2]

Violence, however, is not an end but rather a means for affecting a particular goal, usually a collective goal and is sometimes one of many strategies enlisted for achieving political or social aims within the setting of group conflict. A certain amount of conflict in our society is inevitable because social change occurs mostly through conflict.

For example, Charles Tilly, in examining the relationship between the industrialization and urbanization of the state and collective violence, states that in France, the "long run effect...was to promote new forms of collective action that frequently led to violent conflicts, and thus to change the form of collective violence

---

[1] Lewis Coser, <u>The Functions of Social Conflict,</u> New York, 1956m pp 151

[2] Hugh Graham and Ted Gurr, editors of <u>Violence in America</u>, Vol I, a staff report to the National Commission on the Causes and Prevention of Violence, Washington, D.C., June 1969, pp 2

itself."[3] Tilly disputes the traditional claim that industrialization tends to sharply diminish collective violence. Rather, "collective violence belongs to political life, and changes in its form tell us something important is happening to the political system itself."[4]

Certain theories of social change "conceive of society as an organism characterized by a fair degree of stability,"[5] whose parts are functionally interdependent, much like a human body or an athletic team, working smoothly together for a single, common goal. All of these theories[6] of social change deal directly with the notion of progress. Evolutionary theories describe society as a highly complex organism, with each part assessed in terms of its overall contributions to the survival of society, with stability as the keynote and change occurring only when it directly assures continuing survival.[7]

"Whereas evolutionary theory combines an organismic analogy with the sociological equivalent of Charles Darwin's theory of the evolution of species, equilibrium theorists have limited themselves primarily to the study of the social organism in its environment."[8] Equilibrium theorists see society as an essentially stable, smooth-running organism which also contains homeostatic mechanisms that are designed to restore equilibrium to society once the latter is upset. "Thus, they make explicit the conservative bias that is implicit in evolutionary theory. Social systems change,

---

[3] Charles Tilly, "Collective Violence in European Perspective," <u>Violence in America</u>, Op.cit. pp 28
[4] Ibid. pp 33
[5] Richard Appelbaum, <u>Theories of Social Change</u>, Chicago, 1970, pp 91
[6] These theories include Unilinear theories of social progress (Comte, Main and Morgan), Organismic Theories (Spencer and Durkeim), Modernization Theories of Unilinear Change (Levy, Smelser and Moore), Neoeveolutionary Theory (Steward, White, Sahlins and Service), Equllibrium Theories (Parson and Ogburn), and Rise and Fall Theories (Spengler, Sorokin and Weber).
[7] Appelbaum, Ibid., pp 129
[8] Ibid... pp 131

but only with great difficulty; forces productive of change will tend to be met by compensating forces that offset change."[9]

For many years conflict theory was completely disregarded by political theorists, lending authenticity and support to the other theories previously mentioned and reinforcing the conservative bias that conflict and violence were deviant behavior. Sociologists have neglected conflict theory, "eventually defining it outside the mainstream of American sociology."[10]

As early as 1908, Georges Sorel wrote: "There are so many legal precautions against violence, and our upbringing is directed towards so weakening our tendency towards violence, that we are instinctively inclined to think that any act of violence is a manifestation of a return to barbarism."[11] Lewis Coser wrote that sociologists centered their attention "predominantly upon problems of adjustment rather than upon conflict...When conflict is treated at all, it is treated as a pathological condition which upsets the normal state of community equilibrium."[12]

Talcott Parsons' writings indicate the persistent belief that conflict is dysfunctional and disruptive while disregarding its positive functions and concentrating instead on mechanisms of social control to minimize conflict.[13] But Coser falls into the same trap. In his attempt to discover the functions of social conflict, not only is he rationalizing conflict; he is also channeling and redirecting it into the functionalist's vision of the organismic interdependency of society. As such, Coser believes that conflict becomes institutionalized, regulated and functional in maintaining the stability of society. Conflict becomes an index for stability. But most important of all, according to Coser, conflict and violence lose

---

[9] Appelbaum, Op.cit., pp 132
[10] Ibid. pp 94
[11] Georges Sorel, <u>Reflections on Violence</u>, trans. T. E. Hulme, Collier-MacMillan, LTD., 1970, first printing, 1908
[12] Coser, Op.cit., pp 20, 25
[13] Ibid. pp 23

their essential characteristic: the ability to initiate and affect social change.

Through the functionalist's approach, conflict becomes, instead, a homeostatic mechanism, carefully controlled by the other norms of society. "…we come to see that the multiple group affiliations of individuals make for a multiplicity of conflicts crisscrossing society. Such segmental participation then can result in a kind of balancing mechanism…The interdependence of conflicting groups…provides…[a] check against basic consensual breakdown in an open society."[14] The results lead us back to the difference between the basic premise behind the attitude society takes toward social conflict and violence.

Conflict and political violence have been a repetitive occurrence in American society ever since the 17th century when the original 13 colonies were chartered by England. Instead of trying to treat the subject as if it did not exist, or grasping for rationalizations and excuses when it does occur, researchers must ask more relevant questions. "We must also shift our emphasis from theories which conceive of the 'social structure in terms of a functionally integrated system held in equilibrium by certain patterned and recurrent process,' to theories which place greater emphasis on the role of coercion and constraint in the political system…"[15]

With so many of our citizens engaging in various forms of group conflict to achieve their political agendas, it is time to take a fresh look at the role group conflict and political violence plays in affecting the issues involved and determine the members participating in the conflict. Most alarmingly, gun ownership and the right to bear arms has become its own political movement over the past twenty-five years. Similarly, the pro and anti-abortion

---

[14] Coser, Op.cit., pp /9
[15] Jack Walker, "A Critique of the Elitist Theory of Democracy," <u>The American Political Science Review</u>, Vol LX, June 1966, No. 2, pp 295

movement has many examples where activists have resorted to group conflict and violence to achieve their political agendas.

While there are many other examples to choose from, I believe it was an ethnic conflict that began in New York City in 1968 that ignited the shifting of the paradigm from labeling group conflict and political violence as deviant behavior to an atmosphere where such actions were to be expected because of the gains achieved. Racial tensions and strife reached a boiling point during the 1968 New York City teacher's strike. Out of this turmoil emerged Meir Kahane and the Jewish Defense League, standing up against anti-Semitism and shouting, "Never Again."

I will explore the formative years of the Jewish Defense League, an organization that made no pretense as to how it was going to achieve its mission.

Ethnic Group Conflict

"The premise of conflict theory is that men are organisms and as such they must compete for access to the resources of life. The struggle for existence does not occur between isolated individuals but between groups."[16] For Karl Marx, the scarce resources were economic; for Ralf Dahrendorf, the scarce resource is power. But these may vary to form combinations, consisting of other resources such as privilege, status or equality. "Thus, it is the task of sociology to derive conflicts from specific social structures, and not relegate these conflicts to psychological variables or to descriptive historical ones or to chance."[17]

Raymond Mack and Richard Synder have drawn up a set of properties which outlines the essential characteristics of a conflict situation. The most relevant are:

1. Conflict requires at least two parties or two analytically distinct units or entities.
2. Conflict arises from "position scarcity" and "resource scarcity"
   a. Position scarcity is a condition in which an object cannot occupy two places at the same time, an object cannot simultaneously serve two different functions or a role cannot be simultaneously performed or occupied by two or more actors.
   b. Resource scarcity is a condition in which the supply of desired objects (or states of affairs)

---

16 Appelbaum, Op.cit., pp 133

17 Ibid. pp 93-94

is limited so that parties cannot have all they want of anything.

3. Conflictful behaviors are those designed to destroy, injure, thwart or otherwise control another party, gaining only at each other's expense.

4. Conflict requires interaction among parties in which actions and counteractions are mutually opposed.[18]

A distinction between realistic and non-realistic conflict must also be made. Coser explained that conflict which arises over an incompatibility of goals or even methods to achieve goals, or an incompatibility of values and interests is recognized as realistic conflict. Non-realistic conflict, however, does not involve specific antagonistic means or ends. It arises from a need for tension release by at least one of the parties involved. The release of tension can more easily be re-directed into other channels and continued long after the original conflict has been reconciled.

"Thus anti-Semitism, except where it is caused by conflicts of interest or values between the Jewish and other groups or individuals, will be called non-realistic insofar as it is primarily a response to frustrations in which the object appears suitable for a release of aggressiveness."[19] In a realistic conflict, hostility is directed at the cause of the conflict in hopes of gaining specific results, and the hostility can be terminated at any point while the conflict is reconciled. In non-realistic conflicts, personal aims may perpetuate hostilities long after the group has achieved its goals and it may take forms and direct itself at objects wholly unrelated to the original conflict.

American society rests on a foundation built and nurtured by immigrants. Upon arriving in America, most of these immigrants form ethnic groups based upon a common origin and cultural background. Immigrants sought out "their own kind"

---

[18] Raymond Mack and Richard Synder, "The Analysis of Social Conflict," Bobbs & Merrill Reprint, PS - 177, pp 218

[19] Coser, Op.cit., pp 49

because they could be trusted and they had the same values as the scared new stranger. These village or regional groupings "in their turn sought protection and some power against the strange world in which they found themselves by banding together, one with another."[20] But it is still interesting to note that long after the fears of the American experience have dissolved, third and fourth generation Americans still closely identify with an ethnic group or geographical area or neighborhood.

Andrew Greeley offers an explanation.   "...Presumed common origin as a norm for defining 'we' against 'they' seems to touch on something very basic and primary in the human psyche and that...much of the conflict and strife that persists in the modern world is rooted in such differences."[21] This inclination to continue such homogenous groupings not only enriches society but also provides for diversity within the social structure, and considerably increases and reinforces the potential for conflict.

Just twenty-two years after Greeley wrote this statement, the Soviet Union disintegrated into fifteen separate countries, primarily because the Soviet leaders underestimated the degree to which non-Russian ethnic groups would resist assimilation into Russian society. Because ethnicity is bound in suspicion and distrust and is an appropriate vehicle through which its members can seek greater political, economic and social power for themselves, ethnic conflict becomes an ideally suited testing ground for our case study.

Greeley states that ethnicity becomes very important "1) when an ethnic group is very large and has great actual or potential political and economic power, 2) when one is a member of a small but highly visible or well-organized minority, or 3) when a sophisticated group suddenly becomes conscious that it has

---

[20] Andrew Greeley, <u>Why Can't They Be Like Us?</u>, New York, 1969, pp 17
[21] Ibid. pp 20

become a minority and is surrounded by many other well-organized ethnic communities."[22]

The activities of the Jewish Defense League beginning in 1968 represents a sampling from a much larger social movement which was taking place within the American Jewish community. The impact of the Holocaust following World War II, including resettlement of survivors to the United States, made the Jews living in America much more explicitly conscious of their cultural and historical heritage. Furthermore, the birth and growth of the State of Israel has continually reaffirmed this consciousness since its establishment in 1948. "Thus, while Jews are one of the most thoroughly acculturated groups in American society, they are also extremely conscious of their origins and history, and even in the third and fourth generations they make greater efforts to preserve their own culture than any other major immigrant group."[23]

One reason for this is the shadow cast by anti-Semitism, a disease which has plagued the Jew for centuries in every land in which they have dwelled. This persecution of the Jew is unmatched by any hatred of any other group. Kurt Lewin wrote in 1938 that: "The Jew might as well realize that these happenings are practically independent of good or bad behavior on his part. There is nothing more erroneous than the belief of many Jews that there would be no anti-Semitism if only every Jew behaved properly. One might even say that it is the good behavior of the Jews, their hard work, their efficiency and success as businessmen, physicians and lawyers which give momentum to the anti-Semitic drive. Anti-Semitism cannot be stopped by the good behavior of the individual Jew because it is not an individual but a social problem."[24]

---

[22] Greeley, Op.cit., pp 23-24

[23] Ibid. pp 59

[24] Kurt Lewin, "When Facing Danger" (1939), in <u>Resolving Social Conflict</u>, New York, 1948, pp 162

Therefore, it is impossible to assume, for the purpose of this analysis, that all Jews are subject to a common fate, whether they willingly acknowledge their identification with the group or spend their whole lives trying to assimilate into the larger society. It is this notion of a common fate which makes the Jews a group in reality. And it is anti-Semitism which provides the basis for many conflicts with the Jewish group and other groups.

To examine the nature and development of group conflict and the impact of political violence, I have selected the Jewish Defense League in order to determine the validity of the following hypotheses:

1) "Violence is more likely when a minority group is not content to accept the designation of low rank by majority groups and when it attempts to redefine the situation to permit its assimilation or equal ranking."[25]

2) Religious or ethnic conflict "is more likely to develop when there are no cross pressures at work within the individual."[26] Dual loyalties have always been a source of conflict for Jews. When a person tries to cross the boundaries of a group, he becomes vulnerable to pressures as an individual which he would not otherwise experience if he were part of the group. What effect has the Jewish Defense League had on such pressures and loyalties? Do members consider themselves Jews first or Americans first? Do opponents of the Jewish Defense League within the larger Jewish group consider themselves Jews first or Americans first?

3) Does the use of violence help in resolving issues and achieving goals? As violent strategies are put into continuous use, do they approach the status of normal political behavior, or are they more vigorously condemned as deviant, both by those who feel its impact and those who use it?

---

[25] Mack and Synder, Op.cit., pp 215

[26] Ibid. pp 216

4) Focusing specifically on the Jewish group, what is the effect of violent strategies upon the small sub-group which utilizes such methods and the rest of the group? Why has the "Jewish Establishment" been vehemently opposed to the Jewish Defense League?

As we shall see, the answers to these multilayered questions are, by no means, simple or definitive. "At some point," wrote Pete Hamill, "when peaceful methods do not work, when bureaucracies close the fortress walls, desperate men turn to violence."[27] Some activists don't even wait that long.

---

[27] Pete Hamill, "Beyond Reason," New York Post, January 27, 1972

Origins of the Jewish Defense League

It is well-documented that the American Jewish community, since the beginning of the second half of the twentieth century, has been at the forefront of promoting programs and legislation to eliminate prejudice and inequality in this country. Long involved in the civil rights movement, Jews have fought for better housing, schools and equal employment for African Americans.   The American Jewish community has provided manpower and money to the movement.   Jewish liberalism became synonymous with the civil rights movement in the late 1950's and early 1960's. Jews marched in Selma, Alabama, sat down in Jackson, Mississippi and rode Freedom Buses throughout the South. Schwerner and Goodman were Jewish martyrs who gave their lives for equality, justice and freedom.

"Through the intensively active decade of the civil rights struggle from 1955 to 1965, the Negro and the Jew were often singled out as a clear-cut example of how white and black could work together opposing the common enemy of prejudice and bigotry."[28] The Jewish role in this struggle was significant because it also provided much of its leadership and direction.

In fact, this became a serious source of tension within the movement. As the civil rights struggle gained momentum and certain levels of success were achieved, blacks began to resent the involvement of whites within their movement. In the middle of the 1960's, militant blacks initiated a "hate whitey" campaign which attacked Jews as a separate group. At a Congress of Racial Equality (CORE) meeting in New York in February 1966, one member

---

[28] Bill Novack, New York Times, October 23, 1968, pp 1, continued pp 32

suggested that Hitler had not done the job well enough. That individual was discharged from CORE the next day.[29]

As early as the summer of 1967, the Student Nonviolent Coordinating Committee issued a newsletter carrying a distorted, one-sided attack on Zionists stemming from negative reaction to the Arab-Israeli war which had just occurred. The Zionists were blamed for the Palestine Problem and the newsletter further claimed that the United Nations had no legal authority to recommend the creation of the State of Israel. [30] A report issued by the SNCC stated that "...Israel is and always has been the tool and foot-hold for American and British exploitation in the Middle-East and Africa."[31]

At the same time, there began a shift in the direction of attack in the civil rights struggle. The movement turned part of its attention away from the South and began to chip away at the Northern Fortresses - the ghettos of the urban centers. Black leaders asserted that the Northern whites were pursuing utilitarian goals by participating in the movement. Northern whites were directing the brunt of the struggle to the South, hoping to preserve and perpetuate their own, more subtle forms of discrimination in the North. It was, in effect, bringing the problem home.

The Northern Jewish liberal almost immediately felt the impact of the civil rights movement's new thrust. In 1966, many traditionally liberal Jewish voters helped to defeat a New York City referendum to establish a civilian review board for complaints against police. The referendum had been supported by the black community which felt it was the victim of a double standard of police treatment and protection, a claim that has since been factually supported by arrest and sentencing statistics and which, in 2015, gave birth to the Black Lives Matter movement.

---

[29] Novack, Op.cit. pp 32
[30] SNCC Newsletter, June-July 1967, pp 4-5
[31] SNCC Report, The Middle-East Crisis, August 15, 196, pp 2

Beginning in the late 1960's, blacks sought to control their own movement, their own communities and their own lives. White-owned businesses in black ghettos were attacked in various manners. Changes were leveled against absentee slum landowners.   A good portion of these businessmen and landowners were Jews. The increasing rate of crimes committed against property in the ghetto caused differing views of the "law and order" issue between black residents and Jewish shopkeepers.[32] The influx of more and more African Americans from adjacent ghettos into formerly all-white Jewish neighborhoods also created economic and political arenas where blacks and Jews competed for dominance, creating fear and distrust.

Tensions further intensified in the urban centers as African Americans sought to enter such fields as teaching and social work which had previously attracted large numbers of Jews, magnifying the economic and professional conflict. Jews and blacks, particularly in the New York City metropolitan area, competed for the same jobs. Blacks sought to push their way into the unions on more than just a token basis. Many of these unions were dominated by Jews. The shift of black militants to the Muslim faith carried with it the traditional antagonisms between the Arab and Jew. "School decentralization, community power, community control, are all seen by some Jews as threats to these systems in which the Jewish professional has found his place."[33]

Following the aftermath of World War II, a sense of guilt pervaded world opinion because of the genocide in Germany. Anti-Semitism diminished and the creation of the State of Israel was met by little opposition outside the Arab world. During the 1950's, anti-Semitism in the United States once again rose to the level of subtlety, becoming more pronounced during the 1960's. It could be detected in isolated incidents: in the black militant press, in the political positions of the New Left, in public speeches and

---

[32] Novack, Op. cit... pp 32

[33] Ibid. pp 32

casual conversations. In the New York City metropolitan area, where almost half of America's Jewish population reside alongside a substantial number of blacks and Latinos, this anti-Semitism crashed through the surface in the form of outright hatred during the 1968 public school teacher's strike.

Charges and countercharges of anti-Semitism and white racism permeated the atmosphere over the issue of decentralization, paralyzing the New York City school system for three months. The conflict crystallized around the Ocean Hill - Brownsville school district, headed by Rhody McCoy, which summarily dismissed ten teachers, nine of whom were Jewish. Ocean Hill - Brownsville was the battle ground for the larger urban problem regarding who controls the schools and the union. The conflict could have materialized under different circumstances. The essential element, however, was the tug of war for power between the black community and the white community. The fact that the union was heavily Jewish only added fuel to the fire.

Anti-Semitic feelings had been fed earlier that autumn by troubles over New York University's appointment of John T. Hatchett to it teaching staff and the anti-Israel position of some black militant students. Hatchett was the author of an anti-Semitic article which appeared in the Afro-American Forum, alleging "...that New York City's public school system was dominated by Jews who, with their 'black Anglo-Saxon imitators,' were poisoning the minds of Negro pupils."[34] Speaking before a packed audience in the University's Chapel on the Bronx campus, Hatchett labeled Richard Nixon, Hubert Humphrey and Albert Shanker "racist bastards." Hatchett was soon dismissed.[35]

In the public school crisis, the United Federation of Teachers (UFT), a predominantly white and two-thirds Jewish

---

[34] Jewish Telegraphic Agency, Daily News Bulletin, Vol. 51, No. 195, October 14, 1968 pp 4

[35] The Author, a student at NYU, was in attendance at the speech given by Mr. Hatchett.

union representing the teachers of New York City, came into direct conflict with the predominantly black Ocean Hill - Brownsville school district. Following the teacher dismissals, the school board denied allegations of anti-Semitism. Mayor John Lindsay, in an attempt to ease tensions, met with Jewish leaders who urged him to denounce all forms of anti-Semitism. Tensions increased, however, when a rumor circulated a report that Lindsay had accused Jewish leaders of complicating his problem.[36]

UFT President Albert Shanker threatened that his union would strike if the ten "ousted" teachers were not reinstated immediately. On September 6th, the union voted overwhelmingly to strike,[37] saying that they would defy any Board of Education injunction. On September 9th, 53,000 of the 57,000 city teachers failed to report to work. The strike ended the next day after the union reached a pact with the city providing for 1) reinstatement of the ten teachers, 2) full pay to 300 teachers that had boycotted the school district on behalf of the ten fired teachers, 3) a guarantee that all agreements between the UFT and the Board would be binding on all local boards and 4) the right of appeal of dismissed teachers be granted.[38]

On September 11th, the UFT executive board called a new strike after the pact was not implemented. Teachers did not return to work until September 30th, after the Ocean Hill - Brownsville school board had been suspended and its members reassigned to central board headquarters.[39] On October 1st, J.H.S. 271 closed after students who opposed the reinstatement of the teachers left the school in protest. Nine students were arrested and ten policemen were injured.[40] Shanker, in the meantime, warned of a third strike if the situation did not improve and if the Board did not enforce the agreements which had ended the second strike. On

---

[36] Novack, Op. cit. pp 32
[37] New York Times, September 7, 1968, pp 1
[38] New York Times, September 11, 1968, pp 1
[39] New York Times, October 1, 1968, pp 1
[40] New York Times, October 2, 1968, pp 1

October 14th, the UFT struck for the third time after School Superintendent James Donovan reopened J.H.S. 271 and reinstated seven principals.[41] On November 18th, all the schools finally reopened.

During the school crisis, "Angry shouts from members of the local community of 'Jew Pig' and 'You will go out in a pine box,'...rained down on Jewish teachers"[42] walking the picket-line. On September 24th, 300 Hassidic Jews engaged in a bottle and rock throwing incident with about 100 Latinos in Brownsville. Police said there had been tensions in the area.[43] Teachers received physical threats on their lives. But the UFT was, by no means, a helpless, innocent victim. Rather, the union skillfully manipulated isolated incidents of anti-Semitism to rally and unite its membership against the black community and the school board. This manipulation was successful in arousing the sympathy of many New Yorkers.

Here we have a clear example of what Greeley calls the acculturation process which involves the process of immigrant groups adapting to their new surroundings. Acculturation takes place more rapidly than assimilation and, according to Greeley, consists of six phases. These are: "1) culture shock; 2) organization and emergent self-consciousness; 3) assimilation of the elite; 4) militancy; 5) self-hatred and anti-militancy; and 6) emerging adjustment."[44]. Blacks, entering the fourth phase of militancy - power and cultural pride - have come into conflict with Jews who have seemingly settled themselves into the sixth phase of cultural and assimilated adjustment. But the situation has forced the Jews to return to the fourth phase of militancy and combat the black community on his own terms.

---

[41] New York Times, October 14, 1968, pp 1
[42] Bill Novack, Op.cit., pp 32
[43] New York Times, September 25, 1968, pp 30
[44] Greeley, Op. cit. pp 31

This situation raises many questions. Is the sixth phase, which strikes a balance between ethnic pride and individual assimilation, so weak and impotent that it leaves the Jew vulnerable to attack? Are Jewish institutions unable to cope with rising anti-Semitism or is the "WASP Establishment" eager to play one ethnic group against another? Or, is it a combination of all these factors? Dr. Judd Teller, a writer and advisor to national Jewish organizations, said that, "Jews and Negroes, caught up in the throes of urban conflict, must be on the alert against white Anglo-Saxon Protestant attempts to regain political power in the cities by acting as brokers between Negro and Jew at the expense of both groups."[45]

Thus, by 1968, New York City found out that it was no longer "Fun City." Battle lines were drawn and the slightest spark could set off a new conflict. In this atmosphere, the Jewish Defense League was conceived and into this situation, the Jewish Defense League flung itself head first.

The historical consensus is that JDL was founded by three men: Rabbi Meir Kahane, Bertram Zweibon and Morty Dolinsky, in the summer of 1968. Kahane headed a congregation in Rochdale Village, Queens and was formerly the director of the Center for Political Studies, a private research firm in Washington, D.C. He was also an associate editor of the Jewish Press, a nationally circulated weekly newspaper published in New York. Kahane had for several years already used the paper as a platform to vent his frustration with the Jewish Establishment's handling of such issues as Jewish poverty, street crime and the loss of Jewish souls.

Zweibon was a New York attorney who served as general counsel and spokesperson for the JDL and was later disbarred by the Appellate Division of the Supreme Court of New York in 1993. Dolinsky was the former United States commander of Betar, a militant Zionist organization, whom Kahane had known for years

---

[45] New York Times, November 10, 1968, pp 85

when they were both members. Their hero was Zev Jabotinsky, a revisionist Zionist who founded Betar and other similar movements to promote the immediate creation of a State of Israel.

These three men were acquainted with many of the problems of the lower middle class Jew who was living in New York City neighborhoods such as Borough Park, Crown Heights, Canarsie and East New York. They were alert to the rising anti-Semitism even before the teacher's strike and "they felt that American institutions and Jewish institutions could not cope, nor were they equipped to cope with it," explained Stuart Cohen, JDL Vice Chairman of the National Youth Movement.

These men saw the need for a group to counter Jewish problems on the street. Kahane was continually in touch with these disenfranchised Jews. They visited him, called him and wrote to him. On June 18, 1968, Kahane spoke to a crowd gathered at the West Side Jewish Center, "...where he went on a tirade about the Jewish establishment, how it had abandoned Jews and slavishly supported black civil rights. He denounced Mayor John Lindsay for caving in to black militants."[46] The next day, Kahane opened an office in Manhattan and went to Washington, D.C. to testify in front of a congressional subcommittee on the topic of Soviet Jewry.

"Kahane observed an increase in action of the Left and a corresponding reaction on the Right. The Nationalist Socialist White People's Party wrote in their newsletters that 'The Jews are doing this, they are doing that,' and they played up the image of the dirty Jew. Right now there is a strong Renaissance Party in New York City. The Jew has to worry about the Right, not the Left," continued Cohen.

In 1968, certain tangible variables could be noted: Fear, frustration, anger and discontent with the political status quo.

---

[46] Gal Beckerman, When They Come For Us, We'll Be Gone, Houghton Mifflin Harcourt, 2010, pp 156

These variables reinforce a feeling of collective deprivation which can be defined as a group's "perception of discrepancy between its value expectations and its value capabilities."[47] The urban Jewish population feels that it has reached a certain level and hopes to continue such progress socially and economically. "Value expectations are the goods and conditions of life to which people believe they are rightfully entitled. Value capabilities are the goods and conditions they think they are capable of getting and keeping."[48] The urban Jew feels hindered by the black who is trying to raise himself. The Jew feels it is his attainments; that the black is even trying to pull the Jew down to a lower level. "Look what he is doing to us, after all that we've done for him."

Violence is relevant to collective deprivation as other courses of action become ineffective in acquiring or maintaining desired conditions and goods. In such a context, violence becomes a "last straw" course of action, as other strategies fail and as deprivation intensifies. As a consequence, frustration magnifies with the inability to cope with the problem. The "assumption is that much aggression occurs as a response to frustration...The disposition to respond aggressively when frustrated is part of man's biological makeup..."[49] The Jew is trying to shake the black off his back, but has not been able to do it. In other words, how long can the suburban exodus remain a viable escape? On the other hand, "When the value directly at stake is life, violent response occurs as a reaction to fear rather than expression to anger."[50]

The events leading up to the 1968 teacher's strike and the resulting hostility which boiled to the surface contributing both to the fear and anger that enveloped New York society can be characterized under the heading of "Urban Crisis." Many Jews

---

[47] Ted Gurr, <u>Why Men Rebel</u>, Princeton, New Jersey 1970, pp 26, 29

[48] Gurr, Op.cit., pp 26, 29

[49] Ibid. pp 33

[50] Bryant Wedge, "The Case Study of Student Political Violence: Brazil 1964 and the Dominican Republic, 1965," <u>World Politics</u>, Vol. XXI (Jan. 1969) pp 195-196

abandoned the city by moving to the suburbs. Others turned to the JDL for help.

The Jewish Defense League was in touch with the teachers and offered to escort them to and from school. Many teachers accepted their offer. By Halloween eve, with a membership of a few hundred individuals, the JDL was ready to demonstrate to New Yorkers what it meant by "Never Again."

"The scene: Montefiore Cemetery in the Bronx, where for years Jewish gravestones had been overturned by vandals. On this night, 50 JDL Jews, armed with chains and clubs, 'guarded' the cemetery. Sure enough, some blacks showed up, the Jews stood them off, and the newspapers the next day might as well have carried JDL membership coupons."[51] Such was the beginning of the Jewish Defense League.

The stated aims of the JDL were to teach self-defense, come to the aid of any Jew who was in trouble and to instill Jewish pride. The JDL did face one methodological danger and its critics gnawed at it repeatedly: "if frustration continues, aggression is likely to recur. If it is reduced as a result of the attack, the tendency to attack is reinforced, and the onset of anger in the future is increasingly likely to be accompanied by aggression."[52] The inherent danger is that it becomes convenient to superficially test all other possible alternatives or to submit categorically to outright abandonment of all other alternatives and consistently embrace violence because of expediency and past success. This is a problem which will be explored further on.

"The JDL came into being to physically defend Jews...When people think of Jewish defense, they automatically think of physical assault. And that's not all we meant when we spoke of Jewish defense...It also came into being to go out among Jews and

---

[51] Mel Ziegler, "The JDL and Its Invisible Constituency," New York Magazine, April 1971, pp 30
[52] Gurr, Op.cit., pp 34

instill pride, to defend Jews from simply fading out," explained Kahane.[53] A JDL newsletter stated: "JDL believes in creating a physically strong, a fearless and courageous Jew who fights back. We train ourselves in martial arts because it is better to know how and not have to, than to have to and not know how…Violence is a bad thing, but sometimes necessary." "We don't go out looking to bust heads. We always try to find every single method before using force," explained Cohen. The JDL newsletter also made another interesting point. "The JDL's militancy acts as a gadfly to the moderate and pushes the moderate groups into actions which they would otherwise not take."

A JDL advertisement which appeared in the New York Times on June 24, 1969, stated: "Maybe there are times when there is no other way to get across to the extremist that the Jew is not quite the patsy some think he is. Maybe there is only one way to get across a clear response to people who threaten seizure of synagogues and extortion of money. Maybe nice Jewish boys do not always get through to people who threaten to carry teachers out in pine boxes and to burn down a merchant's store…Maybe in times of crisis Jewish boys should not be that nice."

---

[53] Walter Goodman, "Kahane says: 'I'd love to see the JDL fold up, but'" New York Times Magazine Section, November 21, 1971, pp 33

Crime and Black-Jewish Relations

While it later broadened its scope of activities to include such issues as Soviet Jewry and Arab guerilla hostilities, the JDL's underlying strength in its early years rested as much in its ability to deal effectively with street crime in predominantly Jewish neighborhoods as it did from the resulting impact of such actions: calming the fears of these residents and gaining their trust and confidence, because these Jews had somebody to fall back on when they were threatened.

The JDL was most effective in neighborhoods that were being pressured and surrounded by an influx of blacks and Latinos who were trying to escape the prison walls of their own ghettos. Although the JDL proclaimed to be fighting anti-Semitism in New York, the issue boiled down to an ethnic conflict between blacks and Jews which manifested itself in two forms: street crimes, muggings and burglary against Jewish individuals and businesses, which is a problem not uncommon to most urban areas; and the more specific ethnic attacks against symbols of the ethnic group, i.e. synagogues, religious schools, cemeteries, etc. Both forms of the conflict arose out of basic distrust, competition for community control and power, school control, business dealings and housing.

When a black student, appearing on New York radio station WBAI's Julius Lester Show, said, "As far as I am concerned, more power to Hitler. He didn't make enough lampshades out of them,"[54] and when, just a few days later, New York City schoolteacher Leslie Campbell read an anti-Semitic poem dedicated to Albert Shanker over the same radio station, the JDL

---

[54] Roy Bongartz, "2. Superjew," Esquire Magazine, August, 1070, pp 126

initiated court action in January 1969 for the purpose of forcing the Board of Education to dismiss Campbell.

A few days later, the JDL picketed the radio station, demanding cancellation of the Lester show and demanding an apology from WBAI for its "insensitivity and compliance." WBAI refused to adhere to the demands. When the Metropolitan Museum of Art presented the "Harlem On My Mind" exhibit, the JDL picketed outside, protesting an alleged anti-Semitic catalogue which introduced the exhibition.[55] The catalogue was amended. In February, League members demonstrated outside the Manhattan Center carrying signs which read "Community Control Means Racist Control" while supporters of community control met inside.

During the winter months of 1969, JDL armed street patrols cruised through Jewish neighborhoods equipped with two-way walkie talkies, checking on businesses and Yeshivas (religious schools) in the Bronx, Brooklyn and lower Manhattan, while foot patrols searched for muggers. Kahane explained the reasons for the patrols. "The police can't watch every store. Either the Jew is burned out or we put an armed man in there with the merchant."[56] In dealing with threats of extortion in exchange for protection, Kahane said, "If we know the group, a visit is paid. We'll tell him he should pray for the storekeeper because if the storekeeper's leg is broken, even fifty miles away, we will break your head. It's not nice, but it's language they understand."[57] It is important to remember this statement because it gives a strong indication to the strategy of the JDL. Talking violently, using violent, threatening language to get a message across can be just as effective as employing actual violence.

---

[55] Rudy Johnson, <u>New York Times</u>, January 20, 1969, pp 22

[56] John Peterson, "Camp Builds Cadre of Street Fighters," <u>National Observer</u>, July 28, 1969, JDL reprint, no page number available

[57] Bongartz, Op.cit., pp 127

The JDL, with its street patrols, transformed an urban problem into a Jewish problem. In answer to his Jewish critics who claim that crime is not a Jewish problem, Kahane replied: "So we find assaults on merchants who are predominantly Jewish do not comprise a Jewish issue; that reverse discrimination and quotas that effectively hit Jewish students, businessmen and workers more than other are not really a 'Jewish' problem: that crimes in Jewish neighborhoods are not really aimed at the Jew as such and is therefore not a 'Jewish' problem. If Jews, as part of a general injustice, or general harassment or general persecution, suffer - that is a Jewish problem precisely because Jews are involved. Whether de jure or de facto, it is immaterial to the sensitive Jew..."[58]

In May 1969, the JDL sent about 30 of its members to Temple Emanuel of Fifth Avenue to prevent black militant James Forman from entering the synagogue and disrupting services. Forman had made similar appearances at a few New York churches demanding reparations for alleged exploitation and injustices by the white man against the black and Rabbi Nathan Perlman was going to allow him to speak to his congregation.

"We could not allow that," said Murray Schneider, one of the JDL's chapter coordinators. "Reparations imply guilt, and the Jew has always felt his moral obligation to the black man. Heads would have been broken if Foreman had shown. We felt that if they could extort money from one synagogue, Black extremists all over the country would do the same thing. If they can enter our synagogues, it is just as well that they bring on the machine guns now."[59] The fear of the black was a very real fear, not only of the League but of many non-members in the Jewish community.

But why stand in front of a synagogue with bats and chains? Kahane explained: "We didn't need all these people with their baseball bats. We could have done it much more easily with

---

[58] Meir Kahane, <u>Never Again</u>, Los Angeles, 1971, pp 44
[59] Peterson, Op.cit. no page available

less people. The reason was, we knew there were a lot of people watching us on television and we wanted to get an idea across about the Jewish boy...baby, there's a new Jew."[60] The JDL has used the "show of force" tactic very successfully to its advantage, in most cases to forestall an actual use of force. By creating an image of "the new Jew" and burying the image of the Jewish patsy, the JDL has instilled a certain amount of fear in its enemies, whether it be the local black neighborhood gang or the white neo-Nazi Renaissance Party, where no fear existed before.

Kahane, speaking at a small synagogue in Manhattan, was even more explicit in revealing his strategy: "We have a reputation, spread by our enemies, that we are Jewish Panthers and vigilantes and the more those adjectives spread, the safer you are."[61] "Jewish leaders were horrified by the appearance of these Jewish gang members...Kahane knew that he had stabbed the Jewish establishment where it hurt most: their respectability."[62]

A week after the Temple Emanuel incident, the JDL obtained a court order that required Dr. Beull G. Gallagher, then president of the City College of New York, to reopen the school after 150 Black and Latino students seized eight of the CCNY's 22 buildings, shutting off the South campus. The campus JDL chapter then successfully stalled efforts by Blacks to close the school a second time.

Animosity between blacks and Jews continued. During an election of directors of a Model Cities program who would distribute poverty funds in the Crown Heights section of Brooklyn, the Jewish Community Council received threats that if Jews voted, they would be killed. "Now, whether these threats were real or not, they thought they were real. They were so sure they were real that they said, 'We're not voting'," emphasized Kahane. These people said to the JDL, "For God's sake, come down and help us."

---

[60] Bongartz, Op.cit, pp 110
[61] Ibid., pp 110
[62] Beckerman, Op. cit. pp 158, 159

"So our people took off from work and from school and they stood in Crown Heights at every polling place and they said, 'Let everybody come and vote, black and white and Jew and non-Jew, s is America.'"[63]

Sixteen of 24 Jewish candidates were elected where a year before no Jew was elected. When Sonny Carson (a CORE leader in Brooklyn) took over a Crown Heights Jewish Corporation meeting and started pounding on the table and making demands, residents called upon the JDL. "Now, how do you get Sonny Carson out, especially when Jews are terrified...You don't sit down with Sonny Carson. Sonny Carson does not listen. With Sonny Carson, you walk in and you say, 'Sonny, baby, you gonna get out? Or do we have to cut you up?' And he says, 'Now man, now sit down, let's talk. Now we understand. Now we're speaking Panther to Panther,'" explained Kahane.[64]

---

63 Beckerman, Op.cit., pp 126
64 Goodman, Op.cit., pp 117

Street Patrols – Image of the "New Jew"

During the summer of 1969, the JDL opened a camp in the Catskill Mountains where teenagers were instructed in karate, hand to hand combat, and the use of firearms. They also attended classes on the ideology of the Black Panthers and the Minutemen. Following a visit to the camp in July 1969, John Peterson wrote that the teenagers were participating because they believe "Jews in the United States are fighting for survival...the JDL contends a defense is necessary because of a breakdown in law and order."[65]

In Philadelphia, JDL members patrolled the streets, led by Rabbi Harold Novoseller, who warned, "We're not an ornery group. We're not taking any crap without handing back a double bucketful."[66] In Boston, JDL members joined forces with a black group called Youth Incorporated to patrol the streets in the north Dorchester and Mattapan sections of Boston where "gangs of young blacks have been preying increasingly on older residents, attacking both blacks and whites."[67] Many Jews were afraid of leaving their tenements or apartments to shop or go to the synagogue.

In August, JDL members went to Passaic, New Jersey to protect Jewish merchants from rioting that engulfed the city, "sparked by the attempt of a landlord to raise the rent of tenement apartments occupied mainly by Puerto Ricans."[68] Rioters firebombed a public school and damaged stores and shops, many

---

[65] Peterson, Op.cit.

[66] Bongartz, Op.cit., pp 127

[67] John Fenton, <u>New York Times</u>, November 28, 1969, pp 29

[68] Jewish Telegraphic Agency, August 9, 1969.

of which were owned by Jewish merchants. Passaic Mayor Bernard Pinck called the JDL presence "vigilante control"[69] and said their help was not needed by the city. "The League regards its readiness to use force in certain situations as one of its virtues."[70] By using the street patrols, the JDL helped to curb crimes in these areas, as well as creating the image of a "new Jew." But the idea of a street patrol also served a third purpose: embarrass the politicians and the Jewish Establishment into taking action.

In June 1970, Hassidic Jews stood on one side of Penn Street in the Williamsburg section of Brooklyn and blacks stood on the other side, throwing bottles, rocks and insults at one another. It was another outburst of the tension which had been simmering below the surface for many years. A Jewish woman who had lived on Penn Street for 19 years said: "This happens every summer. We're not accustomed to it even though it happens every summer. We can't get accustomed to it."[71]

This particular summer, events were exacerbated by a traffic accident in the neighborhood. A few days before, a black girl had been killed by a vehicle driven by a Jew. Members of the community invited the JDL to come protect them and Kahane showed up with about two dozen of his followers. The strategy of the JDL in this particular incident was to stage a rally outside the local police station on Clymer Street in the Bedford Avenue section of Brooklyn, protesting harassment of the Hassidic Jews in the neighborhood by roving bands of blacks and Latinos.

Kahane contended that police had failed to provide adequate protection.[72] In return, the police arrested Kahane and four of his followers for assaulting police, resisting arrest and obstruction of justice. After his release, Kahane charged that police had beaten him and his lawyer, Bertram Zweibon, filed a

---

[69] Jewish Telegraphic Agency, August 9, 1969.
[70] McCandish Phillips, <u>New York Times</u>, June 25, 1969, pp 25
[71] <u>New York Times</u>, June 30, 1970, pp 45
[72] <u>New York Times</u>, June 29, 1970, pp 33

June 11, 1971: Rabbi Meir Kahane of the Jewish Defense League being led away by police after demonstration at the Soviet Mission at 67th St. & Third Ave. (Photo by Keith Torrie/NY Daily News Archive via Getty Images)

complaint with the Civilian Complaint Review Board. Kahane took the opportunity to condemn the Board of Rabbis as a "do-nothing" organization and called on Mayor Lindsay to combat anti-Semitism. "If they think Jewish blood is cheaper than anybody else's," said Kahane, "let them know that Jews can riot too."[73]

In October 1970, the calm again was disturbed when 50 young Latinos rampaged a Yom Kippur service at Temple Adath Sochochow in the Borough Park section of Brooklyn.[74] Toward the end of the service, the youths began gathering in front of the synagogue. When two attempted to enter, they were refused. When several worshippers exited, they were pushed around by the crowd and beaten. Wives going to their husbands' aid were also

[73] New York Times, June 30, 1970, pp 45

[74] New York Times, October 12, 1970, pp 23

beaten. The worshippers retreated inside the synagogue and the youths threw rocks and bottles through the windows. By the time the police arrived, the attackers had fled. The next day, the JDL marched through the streets protesting the attack, shouting "We are Jews and we are proud of it." The point of this tactic was not only to embarrass police but to convincingly send a message to the Latino neighbors that they would have to reckon with the JDL the next time anything like this happened.

Here again is another key to the League's strategy. It is difficult for a small group of amateurs to patrol a large area every night. It is more advantageous, however, to seize upon its limited number of successes in fighting crime and creating headline news to embarrass, shame and pressure the police into providing more competent and effective protection.

It was not long after these protests and similar outcries by other groups of citizens that an extra night shift was added to the New York Police Department over the opposition of the Police Benevolent Association. Rabbi Harold Novoseller, who led JDL members to practice firing their own .22 rifles in a rented indoor range, was more explicit about the street patrols: "We don't want to patrol. We don't want a private army. We want to force the police to protect us, to embarrass them into doing their job."[75]

Following the senseless murder of Beno Spiewak, a survivor of Auschwitz, in his candy store one morning late in July 1971, Kahane announced that he was organizing nightly radio car patrols and posting JDL members with shotguns in local stores in the East Flatbush section of Brooklyn.[76] Once almost totally Jewish, East Flatbush had in recent years experienced a mass migration of blacks and Latinos from adjoining Brownsville. Kahane said, "Although our main aim is to protect Jews, we will

---

[75] Bongartz, Op.cit., pp 127

[76] Emanuel Perlmutter, <u>New York Times</u>, August 25, 1971, pp 18

make these patrols interracial because there are [black] residents who suffer from hoodlums, too."[77]

A few days later, 1,500 people packed Tilden High School's auditorium in Brooklyn as Kahane urged residents to arm themselves. "Every Jew a .22." Kahane bitterly attacked Mayor Lindsay and the police for failing to protect residents and said that the community would take matters into their own hands.[78] In their brochure entitled, "Every Jew a .22," released shortly after the Spiewak murder, the JDL advocated for the acquisition of firearms. "Hoodlums look for easy pickings and what is easier picking than a Jewish neighborhood? Jews as a standard do not own weapons - therefore little or no risk is involved in perpetrating violent crimes in Jewish neighborhoods...If a would-be rapist felt that at the first cry for help he would be confronted with 20 gun barrels aimed at him from neighboring homes, he would not be as quick to perpetrate his crime."[79]

In the last twenty years, Second Amendment rights and gun ownership have become a major political issue permeating almost all local, state and federal elections with the National Rifle Association playing a major lobbying role. In 1971 and 1972 Kahane had the political foresight to bring this issue to the front pages of the New York media, but in a way that benefited his organization and his political notoriety. Actually, it didn't matter if only one Jew purchased a gun. The JDL knew this. They didn't expect Jews to flock to the local sporting goods store to purchase a gun.

Even today, many hold the opinion that, "Diaspora Jewish culture is almost pacifist. And the general Jewish view is that non-Jews play with guns, not us Jews. A home with guns is a foreign to a Jew...as gefilte fish is to a Mississippi Baptist."[80]   But by

---

[77] Perlmutter, Op.clt., pp 18

[78] Perlmutter, New York Times, August 31, 1971, pp 11

[79] JDL pamphlet, "Every Jew a .22" pp 2

[80] Dennis Prager, Jewish Journal.com, August 8, 2012

advocating the purchase, the JDL was adding to the image of the new Jew. The potential criminal won't know if the Jew possesses a gun or not, but in the back of his mind the criminal will harbor doubts. He may think twice. So Kahane shouted it; he told the news media so that all would hear him. "Every Jew a .22" He accomplished without doing and he does without creating and, in the end, he achieved what he set out to do.

Kahane, speaking at a Rockaway, Queens synagogue one evening, asked his audience, "What's wrong with a Jew owning a gun? Is it un-Jewish to own a gun? Will they say, 'If Jews have guns everybody will get guns?' Well, where have you been the last ten years? Everybody else already has guns."[81] On the other hand, does the alleged criminal really stop to think if his victim has a weapon or not? Does the criminal even care? It's almost impossible to determine this. In this circumstance, the citizen may not be any better off than before. But there is one element that the citizen has on his side that he didn't have before and this is Kahane's message. Even if all else fails, he knows he can rely on the JDL. Whether it is beating up a few black toughs or posting armed youths in local stores, the JDL won't let the Jew down.

Even with their use of conflict and violence in dealing with urban problems, the JDL proved adept in pursuing their goals within the political framework by actively opposing John Lindsay's re-election in the mayoral race of 1969. Truth squads were organized to follow Lindsay around the city during his campaign and ask him embarrassing questions. The League sponsored anti-Lindsay rallies and motorcades.[82] In an advertisement taken out in the New York Times, Kahane wrote, "...we indict John Lindsay...for indifference to anti-Jewish hate."[83] As Kahane said, "John Lindsay is a nice guy, but he's not our friend."

---

[81] These remarks were made at the Rockaway, Queens synagogue on March 21, 1972 and were recorded first hand by the Author. Any un-footnoted quotations by Kahane in this book can be attributed to this particular speech.
[82] New York Times, October 8, 1969, pp 37
[83] JDL advertisement, New York Times, October 20, 1969, pp 52

The basic explanation for the frustration-aggression thesis is the principle that anger functions as a drive. In other words, "the perception of frustration is said to arouse anger. Aggressive responses tend to occur only when they are evoked by external cue, that is, when the angered person sees an attackable object or person that he associates with as the source of frustration. This argument...suggests that an angered person is not likely to strike out at any object...but only at the targets he thinks are responsible."[84]

If frustration leads to anger, then was the Jewish Defense League made up of a lot of angry people? Yes and no.

To a certain degree, the people who joined the JDL in the very beginning did so particularly out of anger, but also because of fear. Joining a collective allows people to share their fear as well as their hopes. Each person gains confidence from the other, diminishing the intensity of their fear. When 1,500 people crowded the auditorium of Tilden High School after the Spiewak murder, they were filled with anger and fear. The JDL's purpose in bringing them together was directed at restoring their confidence and hope and alleviating their fears, as much as it was directed at capturing their anger and channeling it into solutions to the immediate crisis.

The JDL's use of group conflict and various threats of violence emerged as a response to threats on the absolute value of life. It was directed at targets which the JDL believed were responsible - the criminal and the police. When conflict and violence is used in this context, it becomes the total context.

---

[84] Gurr, <u>Why Men Rebel</u>, Op. cit., pp 34

From Street Patrols to Freeing Soviet Jewry

"The key to understanding political violence and projecting methods for its management must be found in the dynamics of bargaining relationships."[85] H. L. Nieburg explains that the goal of bargaining is to modify "the behavior of others in order to induce some form of accommodation"[86] and this can be accomplished by the use of "deterrence, compulsion, preemption and provocation."[87] Following its inception in 1968, the Jewish Defense League developed into a potent political organization that made very effective use of political violence.

A bargaining dimension exists in all human relationships. "The very process of socialized learning is one of bargaining...action-reaction, punishment-retaliation, love-hate, cooperation-conflict. Such bargaining is universal among formal and informal groups at every level of social organization..."[88] With this background, we can better understand Nieburg's definition of political violence as: "acts of disruption, destruction, injury whose purpose, choice of targets or victims, surrounding circumstances, implementation, and/or effects have political significance, that is, tend to modify the behavior of others in a bargaining situation that has consequences for the social system."[89]

Violence may often be the last resort in a bargaining situation, but the threat of or actual use of violence has the

---

[85] H. L. Nieburg, <u>Political Violence</u>, New York, 1969, pp 59
[86] Ibid. pp 78
[87] Ibid. pp 78
[88] Ibid. pp 56-57
[89] Ibid. pp 13

potential of changing the bargaining equation itself.[90] Political violence, when coordinated properly with organization and propaganda, can have an effect on attitudes in the bargaining relationship which "will be highly disproportionate to the immediate objective consequences of the act..."[91]

Between 1917 and 1964, the plight of the Soviet Jewish community was ignored by the rest of the world as they struggled to reclaim their Jewish heritage. Dov Sperling, who emigrated from Russia in the late 1950's, told students at York University that until 1956, he did not know there existed a State of Israel. "We don't have any culture, any Jewish school - nothing at all. We are Russians as any other Russians, but in our identification card is written 'Ivri - Jew'. We know we are Jews but what does it mean to be a Jew?...I had nothing to answer against other people when they spoke against Jews because I didn't know," remembered Sperling.[92]

In 1957, Sperling saw a documentary about the 1956 Sinai War campaign. "Suddenly I saw Jewish soldiers and I saw a Jewish general with one eye...You must realize that for us it is a big thing to see many Jews together. In Russia, there are only two places where you can see many Jews together - in the few remaining synagogues or the Jewish cemeteries..."[93]

In 1964, Yakov Birnbaum and Glenn Richter organized a group of Yeshiva University and Columbia University students and together they planned the first demonstration on behalf of Soviet Jewry in 47 years. Over 1,400 students participated in this rally, far beyond the organizer's wildest dreams.[94] Birnbaum and Richter later called their group the Student Struggle for Soviet Jewry (SSSJ).

---

[90] H. L. Nieburg, Op.cit., pp 9

[91] Harold Lasswell, <u>Politics: Who Gets What, When, How</u>, Meridian Books, 1936, 11th printing, 1968, pp 55

[92] Dov Sperling, "A Russian Jew Speaks," <u>OR</u>, February 1971, pp 6

[93] Ibid. pp 6

[94] Robert Ratner, "Israel or Death," <u>Te'chiyat Hanefesh</u>, November 29, 1971, pp 2

The SSSJ fought a lonely battle for five years, until the JDL organized a 100 hour vigil in front of the Soviet Mission to the United Nations, launching its own Soviet Jewry campaign on December 29, 1969. Kahane's interest in the plight of Soviet Jews was ignited by a visit he received from Geula Cohen, an Israeli extremist who was a member of Menachem Begin's Herut Party. Cohen and Yitzhak Shamir offered Kahane resources and training if he would focus his organization on Soviet Jewry.

The League wanted to create a larger stage for their endeavors and taking on the cause for freeing Soviet Jewry was a natural next step in their growth and evolution as a political force to be reckoned with. In fact, once they embraced the plight of Soviet Jews wishing to emigrate, they were prepared to fully engage in civil disobedience and break the law, if necessary, to save three million Soviet Jews. Such commitment to a cause places very few limits on the tactics to be used by the League.

The League was much more aggressive than the SSSJ. During the vigil, three different JDL groups carried out a series of coordinated actions in New York City. The first group painted slogans on a Soviet airliner at Kennedy Airport. A second group invaded the offices of Tass, the Soviet news agency, painting slogans and disrupting activities. The third group rampaged through the Aeroflot Intourist offices. Fourteen JDL'ers, including Kahane, were arrested in all.[95]

The success of these actions set the stage for future actions by the League, each action building upon and reinforcing the next. The League was determined to create disturbances in order to advance their political goals and they were prepared to be arrested for their actions. Even though they achieved a certain level of success with their street patrols, they knew that they were operating within a limited sphere of influence.

---

[95] Irving Spiegel, <u>New York Times</u>, December 30, 1969, pp 46

The League staged numerous protests in front of the Soviet Mission in New York, including a second 100 hour vigil on December 30th to protest the Leningrad trial of 11 Russian Jews charged with conspiring to hijack an airplane to Israel. Kahane was arrested again. "For the second time in twenty-four hours, he was in jail. And he loved it. Kahane knew the cause would benefit. This was action with a clear goal. He knew how to get attention. The problem was finding the right focus. Sitting that night in an Upper East Side holding pen with his young followers sleeping on wooden benches next to him, he felt gleeful at his success."[96]

Hundreds of Jews were arrested over the next three years for: obstructing traffic, disorderly conduct, rioting and breaking through police barricades. Another 1,300 were arrested in Washington, D.C. for obstructing traffic during a rally in March 1971 at the Soviet Embassy. Other protests were held at the Soviet Mission's 38-acre estate in Glen Cove, New York. Similar protests were held by the Boston and Philadelphia chapters of the JDL.

A second tactic was directed at destroying cultural relations between the United States and the USSR. Recitals by Russian artists were disrupted in New York and Philadelphia. In 1971, the Moiseyev Dance Company was disrupted during its performance in Philadelphia when a dozen mice were released in the audience. "The disruption was so effective that it was later repeated by others in a store in Providence, Rhode Island that sold Russian goods. The Philadelphia members also threw marbles on the ice during a performance by Russian skaters at the Spectrum."[97] Sit-ins took place at the offices of impresario Sol Hurok to protest his role in the cultural exchange program with the Russians.

In March 1970, the Soviet Union cancelled an appearance by the Bolshoi opera and dance companies, attributing its decision to the American failure to stop "provocations of Zionists thugs."

---

[96] Beckerman, Op. cit., pp 171
[97] Robert Tomasson, <u>New York Times</u>, June 28, 1971, pp 18

Tass reported: "The provocations not only create obstacles to the implementation of Soviet institutions in the U.S. of their official functions, but threatens to disrupt measures within the sphere of cultural exchange..."[98] A spokesman for the JDL responded, "We will continue to dramatize the plight of Soviet Jews in any way we can..."[99]

These protests and disruptions were purposeful and proved successful in drawing the world's attention to the issue of Soviet Jewry. They were well planned and dramatically carried out and were aimed at 1) straining cultural relations between the two great powers "to modify the behavior of others in a bargaining situation," 2) alerting the public to the plight of Soviet Jews by undertaking actions which would attract the public's attention, and 3) placing the bargaining situation under the light of world scrutiny, minimizing, to a certain degree, the ability of the Soviet Union to bargain. The situation between the JDL and the USSR can be characterized as one of action-reaction, escalation, and attack-retaliation.

When Soviet diplomatic cars were damaged in New York and Washington, D.C., American diplomatic cars and those belonging to American journalists were similarly attacked in the USSR. When Soviet officials raided Jewish homes and arrested 21 persons in connection with the attempted Leningrad hijacking, the JDL stormed through the offices of the Amtorg Trading Corporation.[100] A year later, three members of the JDL pleaded guilty in Brooklyn Federal Court to charges related to bombing incidents in 1971 at the Amtorg Trading Corporation offices and at the Long Island estate of the Russian Mission.

In related incidents, in which the JDL's guilt has never been proven, a bomb exploded in the pre-dawn hours outside the Soviet cultural office in Washington, D.C., bringing a strongly worded

---

98 Lawrence Van Gelder, <u>New York Times</u>, December 12, 1970, pp 12
99 Ibid. pp 12
100 C. Gerald Fraser, <u>New York Times</u>, June 24, 1970, pp 14

protest from the Soviet Embassy: "Such connivance on the part of the authorities has resulted in the not unknown hoodlum and terrorist Jewish Defense League's openly declaring its intention to carry on assaults on the lives of the personnel of the Soviet institutions in the United States."[101] Also, the Manhattan offices of Aeroflot and its travel agency Intourist were bombed in November 1970, and a brick smashed the Aeroflot office window two months later. Three months later, a bomb exploded at the offices of Amtorg.

Before each attack, phone calls were received, usually by news services, alerting them to the impending attacks and ending with the message, "Free all Soviet Jews. Let my people go. Never Again." In October 1971, shots were fired into the Soviet Mission in Glen Cove, Long Island and an employee, Iris Kones, died from smoke inhalation when a bomb blasted the Manhattan offices of impresario Sol Hurok. Kahane and Zweibon denied involvement in both incidents, but police arrested Gary Shlian, a JDL member, for using false identification to purchase the rifle that was used in the shooting incident. Shilian was indicted in 1972 and pled guilty in 1975.

A JDL newsletter discussed the "efficacy and tactical effectiveness" of the bombings and related methodology: "We see that violence is sometimes necessitated by the evil doings of others. However, many ask if now is the time to employ such tactics on behalf of Soviet Jewry. Our answer is - 'if not now - when?' What we see now is the imminent physical destruction of three and one half million beings. The enemy facing us cannot be swayed by words, only actions...how can the shattering of glass and brick possibly be deemed an appropriate response to the shattering of the dreams and hopes and the very existence..." of these Soviet Jews?

---

[101] Richard Halloran, <u>New York Times</u>, January 9, 1971, pp 1

Rabbi Meir Kahane, founder of the Jewish Defense League, arrives at London Airport from New York to lead a demonstration outside the Soviet Embassy in London, 13th September 1971. (Photo by George Stroud/Express/Hulton Archive/Getty Images)

In January 1971, the JDL incorporated two more strategies into its Soviet Jewry campaign. The League announced a consumer boycott against the products of American companies doing business with the USSR.[102] The boycott was complemented by demonstrations at various American business concerns, highlighted by a sit-in at the Empire State Building offices of Mack

---

[102] Will Lissner, <u>New York Times</u>, January 21, 1971, pp 9

Truck Co., Inc. which had disclosed plans for building a multi-million dollar plant in the USSR.[103]

The second tactic involved the harassment of Soviet officials and their families living in the United States where the JDL formed teams to "follow, question and harass." Kahane explained that his aim was to provide a crisis in USSR-U.S. relations to stop the countries from "building bridges over Jewish bodies,"[104] and to make life miserable for the Russians. At a speech given at York University in Toronto, Kahane raged that "...the New York Times bleeds for two Soviet women who sit there and say, 'Our children can't go to Central Park.' They haven't begun to see anything yet. If Jews can't go to Israel, Soviet children are not going to Central Park! If Jews are prisoners in labor camps, the Soviets will be prisoners inside that mission!"[105]

What did he mean by this? There existed between the United States and the Soviet Union a bargaining situation. Their ultimate goal, presumably, was to neutralize each other's enormous power, like a slowly played chess match, thereby ensuring the maintenance of some acceptable degree of worldwide order and peace. One of the best ways to accomplish this goal was to map out roads of communication: political visits, joint space programs, cultural and student exchange programs, economic and environmental agreements - in short, any program in which mutual cooperation could be achieved.

If the Jewish Defense League had attempted to solve the Soviet Jewry problem on Russian terms, at the Russian bargaining table, they would have failed before they could even get started. Instead, the League attacked the bargaining equation indirectly by disrupting the bargaining situation between the two countries, and forcing the two countries to deal with the problem before they could restore the bargaining equilibrium.

---

[103] New York Times, June 22, 1971, pp 22
[104] New York Times, January 11, 1971, pp 1
[105] Meir Kahane, "Jewish is Beautiful," OR, February 1971, Vol 1, No. 6, pp 1, 7

Fortunately for the JDL, the USSR chose to enter the bargaining relationship with the JDL on the League's terms. What else could the Russians do but harass American officials and their families stationed in the USSR, damage cars and property, abruptly recall Ambassador Anatoly Dobrynin home without an official farewell, and stage violent demonstrations at the U.S. Embassy.

For the Russians, such retaliations were childish in nature and hindered east-west relations further. It also allowed the JDL to escalate the attack, on its terms, if the Russians remained intransigent. Kahane was keenly aware of the Russian mentality, noting on several occasions that the Russians were "a pragmatic people. If the Soviet Jews are not worth it, they'll let them go. If the price they must pay to keep Soviet Jews in is too high and they're not ready to pay the price, they'll let the Soviet Jews go...The Soviets need things from the West...Let's make them pay a price."[106]

When the JDL forced the Russians to bargain on their terms - successful east-west relations in exchange for Soviet Jewish lives - it became abundantly clear that their strategies had been successful. The JDL had been trying, without any luck, to meet with U.S. Ambassador to the United Nations Charles Yost. "We knew quite clearly we had begun to win when Ambassador Yost finally called us and found time to meet with us, the day after we invaded Amtorg. Yost said we were hurting Soviet-American relations," reflected Kahane.

The JDL's actions were not haphazard or ill-directed. "Putting the Soviet Jewry problem on page one was political violence, a political scheme, well understood by the Soviet Union. We set out with a political scheme to make the Soviet Jewry problem a Richard Nixon problem," Kahane emphasized. And that's exactly what happened. The most prominent mainstream national Jewish organizations, seeking to distance themselves from the JDL, sent numerous communications to state and federal

---

[106] Meir Kahane, Op.cit., pp 7

legislators, including the White House, disavowing any connection to the JDL and condemning their tactics. In response, a recent group of Russian emigrants living in Israel praised the actions of the JDL in a cablegram to various American Jewish leaders who had condemned the League, declaring: "We are convinced the League's policy and activities are most effective. The Soviet Government should be brought to understand that the liberation of Soviet Jews is preferable to endless international complications."[107]

The JDL's strategy using militancy and violence had important implications:

1) It dramatically publicized the oppression of the Soviet Jew and embodied the problem in the public eye.

2) In 1969, there were only two organizations effectively working on behalf of Soviet Jewry - SSSJ and JDL. Over the next 3-5 years, young activists and student groups in local communities and on college campuses were formed across the North American and European continents to take up the struggle for the Soviet Jew. Major Jewish establishment organizations also became fervently involved, lobbying their elected representatives in Washington D.C. "We have become a catalyst on the moderates," explained Kahane. "Militants have always been catalysts for moderates, pushing Jewish groups to do what they have never done before."

3) The actions of the JDL and other groups which followed suit served to compliment the actions of the Soviet Jews themselves: letters of grievance, scores of petitions for emigration representing thousands of families, demonstrations and even an attempted airplane hijacking. When the Soviet Jew read about Russian condemnation of JDL activities, he knew who his friend was. "Go to the Soviet Union," challenged Kahane, "and ask any Jew the name of an American Jewish organization. If he says the B'nai B'rith, I'll pay your airfare!"

---

[107] <u>New York Times</u>, January 16, 1971, pp 11

4) Most importantly, more than 14,000 Jews left Russia in 1971, as compared with 4,300 between 1968 and 1970.[108] Seeking to improve relations with the U.S., the Soviet Union allowed 32,000 Jews to emigrate in 1972 and that number increased to 34,000 in 1973.[109]

But emigration came with a price. The Soviets decided to impose an exorbitant emigration tax on those Jews wishing to leave, ostensively to reimburse the State for the cost of their education. In reaction to the implementation of the tax, Senator Henry Jackson, a Democrat from the state of Washington, introduced an amendment to a large trade bill that was working its way through Congress which would have given the Soviet Union Most Favored Nation trade status.

The amendment, later known as the Jackson-Vanik amendment banned the granting of such favored nation trade status to Communist nations that placed limitations on emigration. "The Nixon administration opposed the amendment as a threat to détente, and Secretary of State Henry Kissinger tried to bully Jewish leaders into rescinding their support. When some leaders wavered, refuseniks in Moscow, risking arrest for treason, wrote an open letter to American Jews warning them against retreat on the amendment. "Brothers, be strong!" they demanded. That message, coming from men and women facing exile to Siberia, was intended to shame. I was in Moscow at the time, and I brought out the letter,"[110] recalled Yossi Klein Halevi years later. Halevi who began his involvement with SSSJ later switched his allegiance to the JDL, having grown frustrated with the "respectability" of the SSSJ.   Eventually, the Jewish Establishment got behind the amendment and it was signed into law in 1975.

---

[108] Nora Levin, <u>Jews in the Soviet Union Since 1917</u>: Paradox in Survival, New York, 1988, pp 681-682

[109] Ibid. pp 696

[110] Yossi Klein Halevi, "Glory," written November 25, 2010, appearing in <u>New Republic</u>, December 2, 2010

Even Birnbaum had to acknowledge "...that Kahane made lasting contributions to the cause of Soviet Jewry. 'He did heighten mass awareness of the plight of Soviet Jewry in a way that would not have occurred otherwise...'" creating "...strong feelings of pride and identification among thousands of Jews in the USSR."[111]

The movement to free Soviet Jews continued for many more years, but the Jewish Defense League had made its mark in advancing the initial struggle with its strategy being more effective in coordinating protests, attacks and propaganda at the most vulnerable targets within their grasp, while producing results greatly disproportionate to its own size and strength.

"Astonishingly, our petty harassment campaign...created the worst crisis in years in Soviet-American relations. What a joke," reminisced Halevi, "yeshiva kids from Brooklyn making headlines by cursing Soviet diplomats. But that was the point. We no longer were just yeshiva kids from Brooklyn. We were outlaws and power-brokers...The JDL's undeniable achievement was to do precisely what Kahane promised: it placed the issue on page one by convincing a shameless media that the Soviet Jewry cause was 'serious' enough to inspire violence."[112]

---

[111] Walter Ruby, The Role of Nonestablishment Groups, A Second Exodus, The American Movement to Free Soviet Jews, Murray Friedman & Albert D. Chernin, Editors, 1999, Brandeis University Press, pp 208
[112] Yossi Klein Halevi, Op.cit.

Structure and Decision-Making

The governance structure of the Jewish Defense League was a pyramid with Rabbi Kahane at its pinnacle, particularly during the early years of its existence. The next level below Kahane could best be described as a formal hierarchical framework, effective yet not bureaucratic, because of the small size of the organization. Beginning at the top, there was the Executive Board, an International Board and, in New York, a State Board. On the local level, there were District Groups, campus groups and local chapters forming the base of the pyramid. The Executive Board determined the policy for the League and passed it on down through the structure to the membership. All the boards were subordinate to the Executive Board, although policy suggestions could originate at any level in the structure and receive consideration from the top. Local and college groups also had a certain degree of autonomy.

Chapters were formed in most major American cities with sizable Jewish populations: Boston, Philadelphia, Cleveland, Miami, San Francisco, Los Angeles, Chicago, Detroit and Albuquerque as well as in Montreal, Toronto, Israel, England and the Netherlands. But New York City was the geographic center of the JDL. Take away New York and the JDL would find survival next to impossible in any other city.

There were numerous reasons for this. The most compelling were that 1) Forty percent of America's Jewry lived in the New York metropolitan area; 2) the New York news media and publicity coverage was extensive with far-reaching affects; and 3) situated in New York were easily attackable targets for the League. The League drew strength from having such a wide range of targets to assail. Part of the success of the JDL was directly linked to its ability to capitalize on its successes and its efficacy to effectively use the tools within its grasp.

Although the League revolved around Kahane and his leadership, he was constantly surrounded by approximately 100 dedicated loyalists. These included board members, JDL Youth movement leaders, public relations people, legal counsel, fundraisers, security personnel and the people who did clerical work. These were just the followers who appeared at the League's office in Brooklyn regularly, some even daily. Then there were chapter coordinators who were constantly in touch by telephone. Ideas, remarks and thoughts incessantly permeated the discussion and constant chatter in the office. The League doesn't have committees, fact finders or investigators who study problems for months. Decisions were sometimes made in a matter of hours, or over the telephone. The atmosphere reminded one of a farm family, everyone working for a common cause.

There is an image that the JDL operated as a dictatorship with Kahane as the dictator. What he says, goes. No back talk, this is the way it is. Kahane has been labeled a maniac, a demagogue and a despot, playing upon the fears and aspirations of his constituency, just as the fascists played upon the fears of the landowners and small businessmen in 1919 Italy. This was an exaggerated picture of the JDL, painted by the news media and further distorted by critics of the League.

Lew Coser, in restating one of Georg Simmel's propositions, says that "conflict with another group leads to the mobilization of the energies of group members and hence to increased cohesion of the group,"[113] which in turn can result in a highly centralized organizational structure, if the group participates in violent strategies. Despotism, on the other hand, "seems to be related to the lack of cohesion; it is required for

---

[113] Coser, Op.cit., pp 95

carrying out hostilities where there is insufficient group solidarity to mobilize energies of group members."[114]

To a group which relies heavily upon political violence to affect the bargaining relationship, it is necessary for the group to exhibit rigidity rather than flexibility. It was also to the JDL's advantage that they were a relatively small group. For a group which relies upon expediency and swiftness in both decision making and implementation, small size and well-defined operational parameters are desirable. Disagreements and long-winded debates, or bureaucratic red tape would only cut down on its tactical mobility.

A small group like the JDL must rely upon the loyalty of its members because of the high cost-risk of its activities. "A confrontation which escalates costs and risk tends to break down the unity of action...members are forced to make their own assessments in terms of other values which they may not share with the group."[115] Because of the high risk involved in its tactics, the JDL must have complete dedication and commitment from its membership. Dissidence can only have negative effects on the small, militant group. Membership in the JDL was not suitable for everyone. For example, in the New England area, eight chapter chairmen resigned late in January 1971 following the bombing of a Soviet cultural building in Washington, D.C. because they could not condone such violent actions. But instead of falling by the wayside, they formed a splinter group.

The League's identity began with ideology and strategy but the JDL was also very selective in deciding who could join the cause. There was little tolerance for drugs and racism. Members caught using or possessing drugs were expelled from the League. Nor would the League tolerate racism from its members. Those members exhibiting overt racist attitudes were immediately ejected from the League. The JDL was also notably security

---

[114] Coser, Op.cit., pp 95
[115] Nieburg, Op.cit., pp 109

conscious, and Robert Fine, head of security, said that known and suspected informers had also been ostracized in the past. "The small, close struggle group...cannot deal with internal conflict and hence punishes expressions of dissent with exclusion."[116]

When the JDL was first formed, those individuals who flocked to join could be characterized into two general categories. The first category was characterized by people unconsciously seeking a virility surrogate and who found that surrogate in joining an organization in which an outlet for proving one's virility could be found in street patrols and beatings. The second category consisted of those people who truly wished to defend Jews and if they could find an opportunity or an excuse to bust heads, all the better. "A former member of the JDL indicated, "that at the time I was a member, from what I saw, the former comprised four-fifths and the latter about one-fifth. I wouldn't say these people weren't committed but these underlying personality types did exist."

Over the next several years, the personality and character of the membership continued to evolve in alignment with the League's own process of maturation, as indicated by the transition from purely physical confrontation to calculated political violence, creating a more viable, sophisticated, rational and smoother running organization during the mid-1970's. Nevertheless, throughout the JDL's existence, it has often been difficult to entirely control or eliminate the hotheads and stereotypes.

This difficult challenge of self-discipline in an organization where chapters are self-forming and operate semi-autonomously is one that would plague the League for a long time. "In the New York metropolitan area, we have 51 chapters, a little over 10,000 members, a little over 14,000 nationally."[117] The result was a loosely controlled federation where headquarters found it inherently difficult to discipline its members, as evidenced by the

---

[116] Coser, Op.cit., pp 102
[117] Goodman, Op.cit., pp 116

attack on the offices of the New York Board of Rabbis on April 30, 1971.

The purpose of the attack was to punish the Board for not helping another Jew get out of jail. This was a reference to Avraham Hershkowitz who was arrested and had been sitting in jail since September 1970 (and later sentenced to five years in prison) for conspiring to hijack an Arab airliner and falsifying statements for obtaining a passport. More than 20 JDL occupiers broke into the office, barricaded the door and disconnected telephones. Led by Executive Director Lawrence Fine, they scattered files and papers and destroyed televisions and tape recorders. The League demanded that the Board raise bail money and provide kosher food for Hershkowitz after the prosecution unexpectedly reneged on a bail agreement. Rabbi Harold Gordon, executive vice president of the Board, said that the attack was "reminiscent of the London Blitz."[118]

Afterward, the League claimed that the wrecking of the office was a mistake; they had planned to use it as a threat only. In an editorial denouncing the raid, the Jewish Week commented: "The raid on the Board of Rabbis was not, we believe, the mistake of top leadership in the JDL. It was rather the work of violence-prone followers who got out of hand. It was the inevitable consequence of over-emphasis and over-publicized emphasis on karate and physical violence..."[119] The raid also pointed out the failure of the JDL to distinguish between constructive and destructive political violence and the inability of the League, during its history, to intelligently draw the line. Harassing families of Russian diplomats, firing bullets into windows, terrorizing Jewish youths who oppose them or because they are viewed as "Radical Zionists" - these were just a few examples of the League's incapacity to act intelligently.

---

[118] <u>Jewish Student Press Service</u>, "JDL Harasses New York Board of Rabbis" pp 2
[119]<u>Jewish Week</u>, Editorial, New York, May 20, 1971

Who Was Attracted to Join the JDL?

In its initial stages, JDL's membership was drawn from lower and middle class Jewish families who lived in areas of New York City faced with urban problems of crime, ethnicity and community control.   But the Soviet Jewry campaign made a significant dent in the apathetic middle class. "Within months, nearly two dozen new JDL groups were chartered in such suburban, unthreatening places as New Rochelle and South Orange, Lawrence and White Plains. A JDL youth organization even formed in upper class Scarsdale. Much more significantly than these new membership groups, however, was the fact that Meir Kahane, once almost unanimously shunned outside of Brooklyn by the Jewish Establishment, was suddenly starting to get invited - and paid a standard fee of $300 - to use the pulpits of those glittering suburban super-sanctuaries to persuade upper class Jews that violence is not un-Jewish."[120]

As the League began to focus on issues such as Jewish education, Jewish poverty, assimilation and Jewish identity, more of the affluent, suburban Jewish population began to sympathize, support and even financially contribute to the League and its activities. "My guess," says Rabbi Emanuel Rackman, provost of Yeshiva University and no friend of the JDL's, "is that the Jewish Defense League has more sympathizers than the combined memberships of all the established organizations."[121]

It was the youth who were the pulse beat of the Jewish Defense League throughout its existence. They were its strength and its spirit. They were attracted to the group because they were

---

[120] Ziegler, Op.cit., pp 31
[121] Ibid. pp 32

seeking desperately to identify with Jewishness, mostly a consequence of the 1967 Six Day War. They were seeking to channel their activism in Jewish directions. "I believe that Jewish youth sense something in the JDL. It's more than one more Jewish group...There's a qualitative difference,"[122] said Kahane.

The youth were a significant asset to the League because of their dedication, enthusiasm and eagerness. These young adults (high school, college and graduate students) also tended to disregard the high cost-risk inherent in the use of political violence and they didn't have many entangling commitments because of their age. Therefore, they could direct all of their energies and attention to the League. Most importantly, they could be easily mobilized. One New York rabbi who opposed the League did comment that the League could unite people very quickly. "They can get 50 people out in the garment center almost instantly, or 70 college students. They work very efficiently on the phone and they have people responsible for mustering units of several dozen..."[123]

The young people played a significant role in many successful League actions. They were the Jewish Defense League. "Without them the middle-aged group founded to challenge black anti-Semitism ...probably would have already disappeared...They are the bodies and the essence of the publicized JDL."[124] These young adults were searching for a way to solidify their Jewish identity by supporting Jewish causes and at the same time they were attracted to the JDL because they were repulsed, in many cases, by their view of the lack of urgency and/or hypocrisy of the Jewish Establishment.

The issue of assimilation and Jewish identity was (and still is) an urgent one in the Jewish community in America and the JDL was in the thick of it. "Are you a Jew first or an American first? Do

---

[122] Zvi Lowenthal and Jonathan Braun, "Right on Judaism...JDL's Meir Kahane Speaks Out-An Interview" _Flame_, Vol 5, No. 1, March 1971

[123] Michael Kaufman, _New York Times_, May 25, 1970, pp 4

[124] Ziegler, Op.cit., pp 34

you fight for Jewish liberation and Jewish cause or everybody else's causes?" "Jewish is beautiful!" These questions struck at the crux of the controversy. The League felt that most of its support came from individuals who were unequivocal about their identity. Marty Rosen, a JDL fundraiser, stated, "There's a question. We're Jews first. The way America is made up, you cannot identify as an American." Asked what he thought those Jews in the Establishment would answer, Rosen replied, "I think that you will hear 75 percent of the time 'American first'."

One of the primary goals of the JDL was, in fact, to make the American Jew realize that he is a Jew before he is anything else. And the League made a most profound impression upon the Jewish youth. Kahane sensed "that kids come to JDL, not really to harass Soviet officials, but to feel Jewish. He wants to bring in all the disaffected Jewish youths...back to Jewishness through JDL. He wants the JDL to be a group in which they can share in the community...reawakening to their own 'national' culture..."[125]

When more than 800 JDL members were arrested at a Soviet Jewry demonstration in Washington, D. C., Kahane was elated. "It was proof of a new wave of Jewish youth. Here were Jews who were not afraid to do something risky for their own people and go to jail for a Jewish cause. It was the fulfillment of Kahane's Jabotinskyite dream."[126]

The idea of assimilation versus Jewish identity is an important concept. To be loyal to Jewish causes, to even be concerned, one must recognize his/her Jewish identity. It is largely an individual problem and when one comes to terms with his own identity, he can step outside of the limbo state and pursue real goals. He doesn't have to worry whether his Christian neighbors accept him or what they think of him. If one takes hold of his Jewish identity, he can rid himself of the cross pressures and dual loyalties which the larger society imposes upon him. This was the

---

[125] Ziegler, Op.cit. pp 36
[126] Beckerman, Op. cit., pp 232

kind of person that was active in Jewish causes. This was the kind of person who joined the Jewish Defense League. This was the kind of Jew that the JDL wanted to create - not a new Jew, but "the resurrection of the old Jew."

But there was another side to this picture. "As the sixties curdled into the seventies, the teenage boys of Meir Kahane's Jewish Defense League, like many other disaffected and angry young men of the time, found the flash and heat of violence irresistible...The...rabbi seemed barely able to control the resentful young men, many from dysfunctional backgrounds, who swam around him like parasitic fish...But out of the emotions he had unleashed...Kahane had built an organization that claimed..."[127] thousands of members.

"Perhaps the most profound effect the meeting with Kahane had on me was that for a few brief hours, I felt I was unequivocally a Jew, a feeling which has not overly possessed me as of late...Kahane managed to make me feel more Jewish in one hour than they [the parents] managed to in twenty years, the Bar Mitzvah extravaganza aside."[128]

As a conflict group, the JDL exhibited a relative level of consistency and simplicity, important characteristics for an organization engaged in continuous violent conflict. Thus, the structure of the JDL insured it the ability to make firm decisions and expect implementation by the membership. In this way, the JDL was able to sharply define its boundaries, resulting in a cohesive membership virtually free from cross pressures and dual loyalty characteristic of larger, more flexible, inclusive groups engaged in non-violent conflict.

---

[127] Beckerman, Op. cit., pp211-212
[128] Joe Polonsky, "Little Big Jew," <u>OR</u>, February 1971, pp 8

What Drove the JDL Ideology?

Ahavat Yisroel - Love of Jew. The JDL asserted that this was the single underlying principle of the League and all its actions sprung forth from it. It was the essence of the Jewish Defense League. According to the JDL, this love encompasses every Jew, no matter where he may be, what options he may hold, what he looks like or the language which he speaks. These variables are inconsequential. There is only one constant and it is vital: the love of one Jew for another.

Kahane defined Ahavat Yisroel: "The pain of a Jew...is our pain. The joy of a Jew...is our joy. We are committed to going to the aid of a Jew who is in need, without distinction, without asking what kind of Jew he is."[129] The weakness of the American Jewish community, however, was that it had "allowed the concept of Ahavat Yisroel to petrify, and we ourselves have become immune to other's pain, and we fail to hear the cry of our brethren."[130]

Why has the American Jewish community permitted this to happen, if it has truly occurred?

When eastern European Jews came to this country, they were total strangers: their language, customs, rituals and appearance prevented them from adapting themselves into the American mainstream. American society frightened them to no end. Without any options, they clung to their Jewish subculture. After a period of adjustment, they overcame their fear of a new country and they began to observe and imitate the larger society. They initiated and copied, integrating into the general society.

---

[129] Kahane, Op.cit., pp 17
[130] Ibid. pp 71

Obviously, the immigrant's Jewish identity had to be compromised. Many were extremely self-conscious about their Judaism and overcompensated for it by escalating the acculturation process.

The Jew who fled from Eastern Europe to the United States in the late 19th and early 20th century did so because his very existence had been threatened by intense Jew hatred in his old community. This fear gripped the immigrant Jew. He was persecuted because of his Jewishness and only by playing down his Jewish identity could he survive in the new country. American society also places added burdens upon its immigrants - the need to conform - the idea that America is the great melting pot and everybody has to melt. So, the Jewish immigrant assimilated into the larger society. In the process, he had to accommodate his "otherness" before he could adopt American lifestyles. "One could be a Jew and at the same time not flaunt it; one could be the kind of a Jew that America would not be ashamed of...To flaunt one's Jewishness was to invite anti-Semitism and put up needless barriers to success." [131]

The pressure to conform and accommodate was doubly great on the eastern European Jewish immigrant because it came from an unlikely source - the established German Jewish community who had come to America in the early 1840's.

These German Jews had already climbed the American ladder of social and economic success years before. At first, the German Jews tried to ignore the new immigrants, greeting them with hostility and disdain. They were frightened of their new "brethren." They were ashamed to associate with them and fearful for their own hard-earned status and position. But attempts to resettle the new immigrants in places other than New York City were relatively unsuccessful and most remained in New York.

---

[131] Kahane, Op.cit., pp 54-55

The German Jews, who had strived for years to gain respectability and acceptance, were now faced with a mass immigration which threatened their position and security. This immigration seemed to cast a pall around all American Jews. The German Jews were finally forced to deal with the problem because they operated the immigration societies and the settlement houses which received these strangers and so they employed them in their garment factories and businesses and tried to "Americanize" them as quickly as possible.

The eastern European Jew began to assimilate by putting his faith into American values: Education, Liberalism, Equality, Democracy, Secularism, Materialism, Love, Public Relations, and "above all, he paid homage to Respectability. It was of paramount importance that the Jew did not say or do things that might provoke non-Jews and inflame Jew hatred. The image of the Jew was vital, and irresponsible and too-militant words and deeds were liable to upset all that the Jew had worked for..."[132]

Following the end of World War II and with the influx of Holocaust refugees, Jewish identity in this country suffered because of the established Jew's pre-occupation with the image that he offers to the majority Christian society and this pre-occupation has extended itself to all facets of society. Unfortunately, the results have been near-tragic. Rather than achieving total integration, the American Jewish community has developed a parallel cultural structure which actually competes with the established WASP structure.

As stated previously, this is Greeley's fourth phase of the acculturation process. Why then has this parallel structure persisted if, as Greeley believes, the Jewish community has entered the sixth phase of this evolution? Is it possible that Greeley has underestimated the nature of the bonds which unite the Jewish community such as the impact of the Six Day War and the Yom Kippur War or the growth of the State of Israel on the

---

[132] Kahane, Op.cit., pp 62

world stage, or even all the unwanted attention brought by the Jewish Defense League during its brief years of prominence championing freedom for Soviet Jews?

The Jewish community is unlike any other ethnic community. It not only has three thousand years of a common history, religion, language and nationalism, but also the sense of a common destiny. Other ethnic groups may have one or two of these traits, but none have all of them. Only the Jew does. And because of this, the Jewish community will never achieve full integration and acceptance into American society, despite the fact that America is such an "open" society that makes assimilation easier and identification harder. But the "image obsession" has also given rise to a terrible hypocrisy within the American Jewish community, causing the alienation of multiple generations of Jewish youths who have had to reconcile their feelings of Jewish pride and sense of "Never Again" with the "bagel and lox" Judaism of their parents, which the JDL was able to draw upon in building its membership and promoting its ideology.

It is this Respectability component that Kahane and his followers attacked so vehemently for they believed it was the antithesis of Ahavat Yisroel. "The need to win the approval of the non-Jew leads the frightened Jew to do those things we think they will like and to refrain from those things they will oppose."[133]

"Respectability is the hallmark, the key to the Jewish people," explained Kahane to his captive audience of middle class suburbanites. "We have to bury Respectability before it buries us!"[134] But how did the JDL hope to accomplish this? By returning to Ahavat Yisroel. The JDL claimed that Ahavat Yisroel could be revived, provided we followed their formula: Hadar, Barzel and Mishma'at.

Hadar means pride, dignity and self-respect. (Hadar first found its implementation in the philosophy of Zev Jabotinsky, a

---

[133] Kahane, Op.cit., pp 72
[134] Ibid. pp 165

Zionist revolutionary of the 1930's and 1940's whom Kahane admired greatly.) Hadar is the backbone for achieving Ahavat Yisroel. It means standing tall and affirming one's self respect, and demanding respect from others. "Hadar is achieved through a study of Jewish history...Hadar reaches its zenith when we contemplate, with a mixture of broken-heartedness and glorious pride, the stubbornness, this obstinate faith, that never for a moment wavered, that adds yet another dimension to Hadar...That dimension is Bitachon - faith in the indestructability of the Jewish people."[135]

Pragmatically, Hadar and Barzel operate hand in hand. Barzel means iron - Jewish iron. "It means understanding the many lessons of Jewish history...It implies a toughness in dealing with those who would harm or destroy the Jew...It means saying that the Jew is prepared to talk man to man or pig to pig. But - never again - man to pig...When one deals with Esau, he must be prepared to use the weapons on Esau...In short, in the defense of Jewish rights, property and lives, the Jew must learn the art of Barzel, the art of physical self-defense."[136]

The last principle is Mishma'at - discipline and unity, especially in times of crisis. It means concentrating all our devotion and actions to Jewish needs, to the survival of the Jewish people. The Jewish Defense League "is committed to creating Jews who have enough Ahavat Yisroel, and who understand Hadar Yisroel, who are willing to use Barzel Yisroel, and who practice Mishma'at Yisroel, in order that the Jewish people will survive."[137]

But most importantly of all, "Never Again!" - a phrase popularized by Kahane as the JDL's rallying cry to mean never again will Jews sit idly by while other Jews are suffering, whether it be in the Soviet Union or Crown Heights. This was the philosophy of the

---

[135] Kahane, Op. cit., pp 190
[136] Ibid., pp 142-144
[137] Steve Gurner, "JDL: The Philosophy of the New Jews," <u>Kol Bo</u>, February 16, 1971, pp 4

Jewish Defense League: Love, Pride, Strength and Unity = Never Again. "The two word slogan perfectly captured the allure Kahane held for American Jews: it simultaneously stirred the memory of their historic helplessness and unblinkingly asserted their newfound strength."[138]

At face value, it is a logical and rational philosophy. Even comforting to the frightened Jew. It is an ideology that appeals to most and with which few can find fault. But it is also a philosophy which one can learn by spending an afternoon in a yeshiva classroom. This is not to imply that the JDL philosophy was simplistic. It is, however, on a level that evades political examination and methodological criticism. There is not much one can do with this philosophy because it is devoid of any meaningful political content.

Violence is a political tool and often times an effective one. So, we saw Soviet officials followed and harassed, the Soviet Mission picketed and Soviet buildings being damaged and bombed in America. We saw Arabs beaten up and Palestinian Liberation offices smashed. We witnessed armed street patrols and blacks beaten up and on rare occasions, we have even seen suspected "self-hating" Jews intimidated and roughed up. How do we explain it? Love of Jews? Is it Jewish pride? Jewish is beautiful? These answers are insufficient. Introspection, a search for identity and roots, a thirst for Jewish knowledge, a commitment to Jewish nationalism and existence - behind the rhetoric a more tactfully employed political philosophy must exist.

"We organized to make it clear that if the Jew is kicked, he will kick back," bluntly stated Bert Zweibon.[139] "A Jewish boy and a non-Jewish boy have both got to learn the same thing, live and let live, and if they don't let you live, well then, beat the heck out of him until he lets you live."[140] Kahane often told the story of

---

[138] Beckerman, Op. cit. pp 212
[139] Peterson, Op. cit.
[140] Bongartz, Op.cit. pp 110

Moses when he saw an Egyptian smiting a Jew. "He didn't look at this act and say, 'Let's form a committee to study the root causes of anti-Semitism'."[141] Instead, he smote the Egyptian. "An eye for an eye? It used to be that way. Now it's an eye for two eyes," explained JDL security head Robert Fine.

Rabbi Meir Kahane (left), head of New York's militant Jewish Defense League, with Mrs. Barbara Osterman, of Britain's Committee for the release of Soviet Jewish prisoners, are seen outside the Soviet Embassy (in Britain), before handing in a protest letter addressed to the Soviet Ambassador. (August 15, 1971 Contributor Bettman)

When Sylva Zalmanson, who was serving a 10-year sentence In a Soviet prison for her part in a plot to hijack a Soviet airliner, came down with tuberculosis, Kahane said "I know that if Mrs. Zalmanson dies, two Soviet leaders will be killed."[142] "What do we do when we see Nazis?" asked Kahane. "We break their heads open!"

141 Kahane, <u>OR</u>, Op.cit., pp 7
142 Goodman, Op.cit., pp 119

This was the ideology which drove the organization and was accepted without much question by the membership, thereby justifying the actions of the Jewish Defense League. Unfortunately, this ideology was lacking in political depth and this was a grave weakness of the League because it is a philosophy which thrives upon reprisal followed by escalation and more reprisal, something that is very difficult to sustain. It is a philosophy "that looks for self-help rather than formal third-party settlement...On the most rudimentary level, social bargaining is simple physical action and reaction. If you push me, I'll push you back...The formula becomes, 'If you push me, I'll push twice and harder'..."[143]

All this constitutes a type of subculture of violence - where JDL members "become specialists in applying various negative kinds and degrees of negative values. This is the primary cause of the so-called subculture of violence among the young of all social groups and among disadvantaged minorities whose resources and behavior options are sharply circumscribed by...exclusion from organized and legitimate activity."[144] In most situations, this formula can only have limited success, limited potential and limited appeal. It can achieve only so much and then starts to plateau and fade because negative values are being exchanged at the most elementary level of bargaining. It hinders the maturation and development of the group, leaving the group in a very unsophisticated position and, eventually, subject to irrelevancy.

"When positive values are not available as a medium of exchange...the likelihood increases of a continuation of bargaining through purely negative values of limited or escalated physical action."[145] It is a process which perpetuates itself and tends to diminish any chance of rising to a more ideal location in the bargaining arena. In fact, the opposite can occur. The group discovers itself in a pattern on which it has become almost totally dependent. It is almost forced to use political violence in every

---

[143] Nieburg, Op.cit., pp 82
[144] Ibid., pp 85
[145] Ibid. pp 85

situation it finds itself. This was an important weakness of the JDL and it stemmed from the more basic flaw in its ideology. Such strategies leave no room on the bargaining table for substantial compromise or a positive exchange of values.

"When defense becomes an ideology unto itself...it is self-defeating."[146] The only way for the JDL to overcome this issue was to incorporate defense into a "comprehensive ideology of Jewish liberation."[147] Jewish education, poverty and Zionism - the League never paid little more than lip service to a broader perspective. An eye for an eye will always be a very narrow solution.

Yet the JDL, although politically narrow in its ideology, was still strong enough during those early years of its existence to mobilize a small army of followers, creating a cohesive, centralized, militant group. Cohesiveness can only be maintained, however, through continuous conflict and "strengthened by constant emphasis on the dangers of anti-Semitism whether or not it is actually present..."[148] History has proven time and again that such efforts are not sustainable as the JDL ultimately discovered. This ideology, almost exclusively emphasizing the defense of all Jews, transcends individualism for the collective goal, objectifying the conflict and making it more intense.[149] However, for the JDL, its philosophy was so singular that its actions overshadowed it.

---

[146] David Mandel, "A Radical Zionist's Critique of JDL," <u>Jewish Student Press Service,</u> 1971, pp 3
[147] Ibid., pp 4
[148] Coser, Op.cit., pp 110
[149] Ibid. pp 118

JDL's Effect on the Jewish Establishment

The Jewish Defense League has been denounced as roughnecks, hooligans, and hoodlums. The League's actions have been characterized as misguided, contemptible, fanatic and counterproductive, just to mention a few. The JDL was criticized by religious and community leaders, political figures, organizations and foreign governments.

The brunt of this bombardment came from the so-called Jewish Establishment. Just what is the Jewish Establishment? It is a term which has come to mean the bureaucratic elite of the American Jewish community - those Jewish institutions and organizations who claim to unequivocally speak for American Jewry. "These organizations - and there are dozens of them... - makeup what is known as 'The Jewish Establishment,' a high-powered, secular, multi-million dollar amalgam. In terms of their concerns and their high priorities, if not their prescriptions, these organizations speak with more or less one loud voice."[150]

At the epicenter of the Jewish Establishment was the National Jewish Community Relations Advisory Council (NJCRAC; later changed to the Jewish Council on Public Affairs), founded on March 19, 1944 by the Council of Jewish Federations whose mission is to improve and safe-guard Jewish communities in the United States from anti-Semitism at home and abroad.

As mentioned in the previous chapter, the Jewish community developed a parallel social structure which, in some ways, competed with the WASP social structure. At the highest

---

[150] Ziegler, Op.cit., pp 31-32

strata of the parallel structure were these Jewish organizations, whose main purpose was to aid in the integration of the Jew into American society. To achieve its goal of defending against anti-Semitism, the NJCRAC "sought to establish dialogue with other ethnic, religious, and cultural groups. They argued that by ensuring and developing mutual respect across many diverse groups each would be allowed to develop freely while participating fully within the broader society of the United States. They also believed that by being active members in their non-Jewish communities and advocating for ideals mentioned above they were upholding the tenets of Judaism and maintaining Jewish tradition. That only by adhering to such principles Jews and other groups could peacefully coexist."[151]

It is no wonder that these organizations spent Jewish money to assist and patronize non-Jewish causes. Their intention was to secure status, position and prestige for the middle and upper class Jew through assimilation, at the cost of Jewish identity. Hence, "I'm an American first, a Jew second." This was one of two statements offered by those members of the Jewish community not associated with the JDL who were interviewed by the author who did not wish to be identified. The other statement was, "It gives a bad image of the Jew to the rest of society." Why? "Because it only stimulates anti-Semitic feelings."

The B'nai B'rith's Anti-Defamation League went to great lengths to put the lid on the JDL. (Much of the material provided for the author's research was cheerfully and enthusiastically provided by the ADL.) "Officially, the ADL says it's so diligent in keeping tabs on JDL because it thinks the Kahane group is an 'exploiter of fear.' While no doubt it does, it probably also has had a thought or two about its own future. How long, after all, can the

---

[151] Michael D. Montalbano, Guide to the Records of National Jewish Community Relations Advisory Council 1940-1994, American Jewish Historical Society, 2002

ADL remain a $5 million dollar defense group if Kahane can make it look as though he's doing all the defending?"[152]

"The Jewish Defense League is a self-appointed group of vigilantes whose protection the Jewish community does not need or want," said Arnold Forster, the ADL's chief counsel.[153] Samuel Dalsimer, national chairman of the ADL, said, "We find the group's paramilitary operations and sensationalist appeals to raw emotion an embarrassment and a potential danger."[154]

But the ADL was not alone in its energetic assault. The Union of Orthodox Jewish Congregations of America denounced the JDL as "destructive and irresponsible."[155] During the New York mayoral campaign, in 1969, 300 Jewish leaders, headed by former Supreme Court Justice Arthur Goldberg, singled out the JDL, "for what is described as an effort 'to inject virulent hatred and group antagonism.'"[156] Following the Temple Emanuel incident, Rabbi Maurice Eisendrath, president of the Union of American Hebrew Congregations, charged that the JDL was "no different from whites carrying robes and hoods, standing in front of burning crosses."[157] In September 1969, the NJCRAC issued a statement "denouncing the JDL for its 'paramilitary operations' which [it] viewed as 'destructive of public order and contributory to divisiveness and terror."[158]

The assault by the Jewish Establishment against the JDL was, for many years, seemingly endless. Their Soviet Jewry campaign was termed injurious and detrimental to the safety of the Soviet Jew. "The lunatic fringe actions of the Jewish Defense

---

[152] Ziegler, Op.cit., pp 33

[153] Phillips, Op.cit., pp 25

[154] Ibid. pp 25

[155] New York Times, November 26, 1970, pp 48

[156] Irving Spiegel, New York Times, October 10, 1969, pp 52

[157] New York Times, May 18, 1969, pp 81

[158] Jack Wertheimer, "Jewish Organizational Life in the United States Since 1945," American Jewish Year Book 1995, Vol 95, pp 37

League have endangered the cause of Soviet Jewry."[159] Soviet Jewish dissidents such as Boris Kochubievsky, Andrei Sinyavsky and Yuli Daniel, however, had been subject to Russian bully tactics since the mid-1960's, even before the first petitions arrived in the West, and certainly several years before the JDL took up the cause.

In February 1971, delegates from every major Jewish organization met in Brussels to discuss the plight of Soviet Jewry. The conference was disjointed and impotent. Internal bickering and confusion marred its external influence. "The Brussels Conference was perhaps the most telling evidence of the moral bankruptcy of world Jewish leadership since the Holocaust."[160]

The conference finally came crashing to the ground when Kahane, uninvited, flew to Brussels to offer a concrete ten point proposal for Soviet Jewry. He was refused admittance to the conference, despite the protests from a small minority of delegates, including Otto Preminger, Menachem Begin, Paddy Chayefsky and Morris Brafman, who declared that Kahane had a right to speak. Instead, security police escorted him back to a waiting airliner. Upon returning to New York, Kahane immediately called a press conference to issue his ten point action plan, further embarrassing the Jewish Establishment. Kahane also tried to gain entrance to the 1976 Brussels Conference but was denied entry, leading to his detention and expulsion from Belgium a second time.

The question was, "Why?" What overall effect did the JDL have upon the Jewish Establishment that it should bring its wrath down upon the JDL's head?

The answer is that "The JDL legitimized violent responses to anti-Semitism, demonstrating a dissatisfaction in at least part of the Jewish community with the controlled style of the established groups and a willingness to condone even illegal activities.

---

[159] <u>New York Times</u>, January 11, 1971, pp 15
[160] Robert Goldman, "World Jewish Leadership and Soviet Jewry," <u>Jewish Student Press Services</u>, 1972

Through its frequent references to the Nazi era, the JDL also demonstrated how the memory of the Holocaust could serve as a powerful weapon in the arsenal of Jewish organizational life, as an instrument for recruiting followers and a justification for militancy."[161]

During this period of time, the values and priorities of the Jewish Establishment were also becoming the center of controversy from young Jews associated with the counterculture and New Left, separating youth from parent, grass-roots from Establishment.   The derivation of this controversy was an outgrowth of assimilation. In its quest to forge a coalition with non-Jewish America, the Jewish Establishment had, for years, directed its attention toward secular, non-Jewish activities, while almost systematically ignoring Jewish community needs. When Barbara Streisand was unable to buy a $250,000 co-op in New York City, the American Jewish Committee immediately turned its full legal attention to the matter. Why? Because she was of their class and they were fearful it could happen to them.

But what did the Jewish Establishment do for the thousands of elderly Jewish poor who were managing on less than a minimum poverty level? Jewish money was being spent on non-Jewish hospitals instead of Jewish education or day care centers. What did the Establishment do for Soviet Jewry prior to 1970? And of course, the most telling question: What did the Jewish Establishment do while six million were gassed and exterminated in Europe during the Holocaust?

The Allocation Budget of the Federation of Jewish Philanthropies of New York for the fiscal year 1968-1969 reveals some very interesting figures.[162] Jewish education received only 4.9 % of the Federation's grants ($911,743.) Jewish camps (which are secular in nature) received only 4.4% of the Federation's total allocation.   Care for the Jewish aged received only 7.2%

---

[161] Wertheimer, Op.cit., pp 38

[162] Jewish Liberation Journal, April-May 1970, No. 7, pp 4-5

($1,342,224) of the Federation's grants with only $204,522 earmarked for services for the aged. In many cases, Federation grants represented more than half of the total expenditures for these categories, indicating that other organizations were contributing very little to their support.

Where was Jewish money going, then? So-called "Jewish" hospitals received 25.8% of the Federation's budget ($4,811,207.) This particular allocation is difficult to comprehend. What is a "Jewish" hospital? Is it only for Jews? Of course not. They serve everyone who comes through their doors. In fact, they didn't even provide kosher food in most of these hospitals. Another 22.3% was allocated to community centers. Yet this money is not really serving Jewish needs either because most of the YMHA, which once exclusively served Jewish families, now catered to the African American and Latino populations that have moved into these neighborhoods as Jewish families moved out. And when Jewish college students of the New Left sat in at the Federation's New York office to protest the misplaced priorities of the organized Jewish Establishment, they were all arrested. "The student protesters...wanted a greater say in how the community allocated its resources and worked particularly to redirect communal spending toward Jewish educational, religious, and cultural pursuits and away from nonsectarian causes, such as Jewish hospitals."[163]

"We are doing things quietly, behind the scenes." This was the response of the Jewish Establishment, Kahane warned us. "It will be engraved on the Jewish leader's gravestone...People who oppose violence have no great problem of their own until it hits home. It almost always comes from a rich Jew who lives in Scarsdale or some other rich suburb...The establishment Jew is scandalized by us, but our support comes from the grassroots."[164]

---

[163] Wertheimer, Op.cit., pp 39
[164] Peterson, Op.cit.

Kahane charged that the poor Jew was being neglected by the Jewish Establishment because "they are too busy bleeding for others."[165] Moral bankruptcy was most visible in relationship to Jewish education. "It is not strange. The Jewish Establishment is opposed, in principle, to the Jewish yeshiva. It is too Jewish...It prevents integration of the Jew with the non-Jew...The yeshiva is no friend of the Jewish Establishment, because it reveals its nakedness of Jewish soul and its paucity of Jewish knowledge."[166]

The role of the Jewish Establishment in assimilation and anti-Semitism is unfortunately linked. The fear of anti-Semitism has been manipulated by these institutions to gain support for their programs which ultimately strengthen the assimilation process. "The problems of poverty, reverse discrimination and physical assaults on Jews were not new. They had been with us for years while the major Jewish groups did nothing, in great measure because their liberal tendencies drove them to favor an 'integration' that destroyed Jewish neighborhoods, a reverse discrimination that would 'compensate' [Blacks] for past injustices, and also because they had no contact with the masses of poor, struggling, and frightened Jews."[167]

The Jewish Establishment's fear of the JDL was based upon two central themes: 1) the JDL, in formulating its own image of the Jew, undermines the image of the Jew which the Establishment, for years, has labored so hard to perfect; and 2) the JDL threatened the authority and ongoing support of the established institutions. An ADL booklet states: "The good image of the American Jewish community is also at stake. Many Jewish leaders view the JDL as a distortion of the image of the American Jew..."[168]

---

[165] Kahane, Op.cit., pp 10

[166] Ibid. pp 38

[167] Meir Kahane, <u>The Story of the Jewish Defense League</u>, Radnor, PA, 1975, pp 207-208

[168] <u>Facts</u>, published by the ADL, February 1971, Vol. 20, No. 1, pp 524

One could make the argument that what emerged from this conflict was a subtle form of self-hatred among Jews. Any degree of a loss of Jewish identity must reciprocally result from a similar increase in the degree of self-hatred, in relationship to both the group and the individual and may "be directed against the Jews as a group, against a particular fraction of the Jews, against his own family, or against himself."[169] This self-hatred usually takes subtle forms (in rare instances it is direct and open) - a Jewish businessman who goes out of his way to hire non-Jews, Jews who avoid Jewish associations, the aversion of the Jewish atheist to Jewish religious symbols, the Jewish student handing out Al Fatah handbills, or the ADL assisting Federal investigators in the collecting and preparation of evidence against the JDL.

In attempting to explain Jewish self-hatred, scholars have described it as an example of a deep-seated human instinct - Freud's "death instinct."[170] But psychologist Kurt Lewin disputes this contention. "If self-hatred were the result of a general instinct, we should expect its degree to depend only upon the personality of the individual. But the amount of self-hatred the individual Jew shows seems to depend far more on his attitude toward Judaism than on his personality."[171] This attitude is measured by the degree his belonging to the group impedes his personal goals.

While it has improved its position substantially since the mid-1980's, during the 1970's the Jewish community, as a minority in America, could be termed "underprivileged" in relation to its access to the resources, power, prestige and position of the non-Jewish Establishment. "An important factor for the strength of the forces toward and away from the group is the degree to which the individual fulfillment of the individual's own needs is furthered or hampered by his membership in the group."[172]

---

[169] Lewin, Op. cit., pp 187

[170] Ibid. pp 188

[171] Ibid. pp 189

[172] Ibid. pp 191

A privileged group offers the individual more than an underprivileged group. The Jew is a prime example of an individual who believes his goal attainment is hampered by belonging to the group because of the pressure of American society to conform and to achieve. "The forces acting on a member of an underprivileged group are directed away from the central area, toward the periphery of the group and, if possible, toward the still higher status of the majority." [173] The individual who desires to cut himself loose from his Jewish ties and connections will do so by showing contempt and hate for the Jewish community. But because barriers still exist, "the more typically Jewish people are, or the more typically Jewish a cultural symbol or behavior pattern is, the more distasteful they will appear to this person."[174]

It is natural for any minority group to seek its leadership from those individuals who have risen the social and economic ladder of success and who have distinguished themselves and been rewarded with some degree of preferential treatment from the majority. "This places them culturally on the periphery of the underprivileged group and makes them more likely to be 'marginal' persons...Nevertheless, they are frequently called for leadership by the underprivileged group because of their status and power. They themselves are usually eager to accept the leading role in the minority, partly as a substitute for gaining status in the majority, partly because such leadership makes it possible for them to have and maintain additional contact with the majority."[175]

The crisis that faced the Jewish Establishment in the early 1970's, including allegations of moral bankruptcy that arose from its conflict with the JDL and the New Left, can be attributed to its marginal leadership.   These leaders were only minimally concerned with the Jewish community's many needs. "Having achieved a relatively satisfactory status among non-Jews, these individuals are chiefly concerned with maintaining the status quo

---

[173] Lewin, Op.cit., pp 194
[174] Ibid. pp 194
[175] Ibid. pp 196

and so try to soft pedal any action which might arouse the attention of the non-Jew...they are so accustomed to viewing Jewish events with the eyes of the anti-Semite that they are afraid of the accusation of double loyalty in the case of any outspoken Jewish action...hush-hush policy springs from the same forces of negative chauvinism or fear as Jewish self-hatred does. In fact, it is one of the most damaging varieties of Jewish self-hatred."[176] It is this self-hatred which cripples and hamstrings the Jewish community.

"The most immediate and pressing problem in this country is, 'Will there be Jews?' Many young Jews are assimilated. Jewish education in this country is a joke, ludicrous and tragic...We never gave our children a Jewish education. If their Jewish heroes are named Angela and Che, we know who is to blame...Jewish education in this country is aimed at one thing - the Bar Mitzvah. If I had it in my power, there would never be another Bar Mitzvah," promised Kahane.

Of course, it is more complicated than the way in which Kahane framed the issue, but is it so surprising that not much has changed, even 50 years later? The JDL claimed to serve as a catalyst to moderates. Certainly, counteraction by Jewish groups towards the JDL also resulted in the mobilization of other elements within the Jewish community, to a moderate degree, to take positive actions on behalf of Jewish issues. Like it or not, the evidence shows that the JDL had a reverberating impact upon hitherto apathetic elements of the Jewish community, sparking Jewish consciousness and pride among parents and youth alike.

---

[176] Lewin, Op. cit., pp 196-197

Jewish Identity, Assimilation and Aliyah

The examination of the JDL's first five years has provided an excellent example of the role that group conflict and political violence have had upon issues and members. I have demonstrated how conflict serves to disturb the status quo and affect change, revolving, at its most elementary level, around competition for access to the resources of life.

Conflict, instead of being an index for stability, acts as a very important index measuring social change by intensifying as frustration mounts and the desire for change increases while the intransigence of the status quo continues.

Returning to Mack and Synder's hypothetical model for conflict, the Jewish Defense League classically meets the requirements which the model sets forth: 1) The JDL's conflict with the black community arose from position scarcity and resource scarcity; 2) Conflictful behaviors were used by the JDL "designed to destroy, injure, thwart or otherwise control another party" and; 3) The conflict involved mutually opposed actions, whether they be by the Soviet Union or the New York Federation of Philanthropies.

The actions of the JDL have shown that "violence is more likely when a minority group is not content to accept the designation of low rank by majority groups...and is more likely to develop when there are no cross pressures at work within the individual."[177] The nature of ethnic conflict suggests that it has inherent properties which act as variables which are not present in other types of conflict. As the actions of the Jewish Defense

---

[177] Mack and Synder, Op.cit., pp 215-216

League illustrate, ethnic conflict draws strength from a sense of pride and loyalty, a common heritage and a common goal. The fundamental goal of the group is to survive as a group, usually emanating in a more militant stance. The group also serves to clarify the individual's goals and transform them into the collective goal much more successfully than a non-ethnic group.

In the first chapter, conflict which was derived from anti-Semitism was questioned for its "realistic" content. The Jewish Defense League engaged in realistic conflict because the anti-Semitism that it dealt with was caused by conflicts of interest and values, and not as a response to frustrations in which the Jew appears as a suitable object for release of aggressiveness.

The intensity of the ethnic conflict is also subject to the complexity of an internal struggle between asserting a positive identity and assimilation. It can be argued that the American community and the Jewish community, despite its vigorous attempts to assimilate, have discovered that a singular existence for the two groups is incompatible, unobtainable and, in certain instances, undesirable. Those who find assimilation undesirable are part of the new social trend that developed among many members of the American Jewish community. This movement was only in its infancy in the 1970's, but it had already shaken the very pillars which support the American Jewish lifestyle.

This was the chord of discontent which the Jewish Defense League struck. This was the larger social movement of which the JDL became a part of. The assimilated Jews have actually been wedged into the middle of the "privileged" and "underprivileged" groups by their attempts to assimilate. This struggle between assimilation and positive Jewish identity will determine the future of the American Jewish community.

Such issues as the apathy and moral bankruptcy of the Jewish Establishment, of Jewish poor and even Soviet Jewry, have only short-range appeal. The influx of young, talented leadership into the established Jewish institutions in the late 1970's was starting to show profitable returns as the Establishment reordered its priorities. Major groups were finally trying to alleviate Jewish poverty and even the Soviet Union indicated that Jewish emigration would continue.

Even so, we must look beyond these issues and inevitably ask ourselves, "What does the future hold for the American Jewish community?" The JDL claimed that anti-Semitism was on the rise in America as evidenced by the increasing activity of many neo-Nazi and white supremacy groups across the country. In California, the JDL joined forces with Blacks and Chicanos and other Christian groups to rout a Nazi group from their Los Angeles suburb. The JTA reported that "The Nazi headquarters...is occupied by some 25 uniformed 'storm troopers,' most of whom are under 25 years of age, who sell and distribute party literature, including copies of Mein Kampf."[178] Sheldon Davis, editor of the JDL newsletter, said during a speech at New York University, that a group in Virginia had actually built a gas chamber hoping to use it for Jews. "It somehow got blown up. Maybe it was a gas leak," hinted Davis.

A swing of the middle class to the political right began during the 1970's, something feared by many in the ranks of the Jewish community. The Jewish Defense League attempted to capitalize on this swing, with only nominal success, as Kahane took up the torch to warn his fellow Jews. He said, "America has been a good country to the Jewish people, but its faults must be changed...We're facing a terrible crisis, an impending holocaust. The people who voted for [George] Wallace (in the 1968 presidential election and the 1972 primary election) are ordinary people. But the racial situation has gotten worse. There is such a thing as rising expectations. The black man wants what every white man wants - more. Busing is not something we can laugh at. It is a serious problem. In high school after high school there are racial conflicts. Most Jews live in intellectual ghettos. People in this country speak of gas chambers and we say it can't happen here. Our leaders play number games - 'How many members do

---

[178] Leslie Goldberg, <u>Jewish Telegraphic Agency</u>, January 26, 1972, pp 1

they have? They (the white supremacists) can't do anything. They're too small.'" It's unfortunate, but not surprising how much the 2020 presidential election mirrored in many ways the rhetoric of the 1968 campaign, drawing on the same racial fears that still exist today.

Much of the literature of the radical right is full of Jew hatred. During the 1970's and 1980's, other elements of this society blamed the Jew for the American failure in Vietnam while the New Left pleaded that the Middle East should not become the next Southeast Asia.[179] As the Vietnam War unwound, inflation and unemployment continued. Who will be blamed? The Jew, of course, answered Kahane. "People who are frightened of their economic future are desperate people, and desperate people are dangerous."[180] "We have become conditioned to thinking of a white backlash in terms of poorer, lower-class, blue-collar whites turning against blacks. What we do not contemplate is an alliance of these lower classes, white and black, turning against the Jews."[181]

While Kahane proved to be very perceptive, he was not always prophetic. Although black anti-Semitism has been the source of much anxiety in the Jewish community, the black-Jewish conflict in New York City subsided beginning in the 1990's once the anti-Semitism preached by Louis Farrakhan, founder of the Nation of Islam, diminished when he turned his focus to other issues and when Kahane was assassinated in 1990. "The fear that African American anti-Semitism might spread from individual racists to infect broad segments of academia, the civil rights movement, and even the political sphere appears to have been unrealistic."[182]

---

[179] In early 1972, an advertisement appeared in the New York Times to this effect.

[180] Kahane, <u>Never Again</u>, Op.cit., pp 91

[181] Ibld. pp 104

[182] Jerome A. Chanes, "Blacks and Jews in America: History, Myths, and Realities," <u>Jerusalem Center For Public Affairs</u>, March 15, 2006

Yet Kahane projected his personal fears onto and through the Jewish Defense League, believing that the Jew was the most hated group in America. He claimed that American institutions were reviving quota systems for the Jews in colleges, in civil service positions and in the distribution of anti-poverty funds. Still, the "mainstreaming" of anti-Semitism in this country has not occurred. "Although blacks do continue to be relatively more anti-Semitic than whites at any given educational level, that is not the same as saying they become more anti-Semitic with higher education and economic status. On the contrary, they become less anti-Semitic, as do other members of the society."[183]

Notwithstanding this evolving trend, Kahane's answer was Aliyah, starting with his own decision to emigrate to Israel with his family in 1971. Shmuel Shoshan, the JDL National Director of Public Relations, implored his readers to "liquidate the American exile before it liquidates you...What American Jewry needs is a greater capacity to develop articulated fears that match the magnitude of tomorrow's danger..."[184] Herein resided the JDL's reason for promoting Aliyah. Once again, the League's strategy struck a note of consistency by appealing to negative values rather than positive values. The League hoped to convince Jews to move to Israel by stirring up images of impending disaster and holocaust. "...stake out a new frontier...where a Jew can live as a Jew - where your children will never be beaten because they are Jewish...where no one will ever yell 'kike!'..."[185]

The American Jewish community appears to be entrenched here, and despite all of Kahane's prophesizing, it seems very unlikely that there will be any mass Aliyah taking place anytime soon. In fact, results so far have been negligible. Between 1948 and 2013, the total number of North American Jews making their way to the holy land is about 140,000,[186] an average of 2,200

---

[183] Chanes, Op.cit.
[184] Shmuel Shoshan, "Jew Go Home" pp 2 (JDL pamphlet)
[185] JDL newsletter, "Jews - Go Home - A Case for Aliyah" pp 3
[186] JewishVirtualLibrary.org

per year. The vast majority of these are young couples, many of whom have grown disenchanted with the American situation.

For centuries, wherever the Jew has dwelled in the Diaspora, he has avoided confrontations with his neighbors and enemies, retreating instead and surviving because of it. In many instances, he bought and bribed other people in exchange for protection. When one ally failed him, he sought out another.

But the Jew always backed away from engaging his antagonist. It became a way of life for the Jew. To do otherwise meant extinction. The cost-risk was too high. Turning the other cheek worked well for the Jew until Hitler came into power. Running away, even becoming oblivious through assimilation, backfired in the Jew's face because this time he had no allies. He couldn't even buy protection, as documented by the movie, "Shop on Main Street," a 1965 Czechoslovak film about the Aryanization program during World War II. With so much unrest around the world, only if the situation in America becomes unbearable for the Jew and he is forced to flee will he go to Israel, (there is some evidence of that very phenomena taking place most recently in France, where French Aliyah set new records in 2014 and 2015).

The lessons of World War II indicated that a new policy for survival had to be implemented. The social movement of the Jewish community during the 1970's produced conflict both within the group and between various elements of the group and the larger society. The Jewish Defense League "stands out only as the first noisy manifestation..."[187] of this social movement. There were large numbers of Jews who willingly regarded themselves as positively and militantly Jewish without associating with the JDL. Such is the struggle that took place between the Jewish Establishment and young Jews seeking change. No longer would turning the other cheek work. The answer, and one of the few areas of common ground between the Jewish Left and Right, was to stand up proudly and claim your identity.

---

[187] Ziegler, Op.cit., pp 36

Cracks in the Armor

It's not surprising that after several years, cracks in the JDL's armor began to appear both from within and from outside. Government authorities began to bear down on the League. Many Jewish groups began demanding that the New York Police Department "use their full powers to end the terrorist activities encouraged by, or committed by the Jewish Defense League by seeing to it that those responsible for such crimes of violence suffer the full penalty of the law."[188]

Seven JDL members faced prison terms in connection with the invasion of the Amtorg offices and several served prison time. Two members were convicted in 1973 for the bombing of a Los Angeles apartment building. In 1971, a dozen more members, including Kahane, were charged with conspiring to manufacture explosives and with violating the Federal Gun Control Act of 1968. Of this group, Kahane and two others pleaded guilty and received suspended sentences and probation. Kahane immediately moved with his family to Israel, but later violated his probation and in 1975, spent a year in prison.[189]

In 1974, a leader of the Pennsylvania JDL was convicted in connection with the disruption of the Bolshoi Ballet at Temple University and another leader was arrested by the FBI and convicted in connection with assassination threats on Palestinian leader Yasir Arafat. In 1975, two more members on the West Coast pleaded guilty to firebombing a car belonging to a Nazi sympathizer. Many more were arrested or indicted during this time.

---

[188] <u>Jewish Telegraphic Agency</u>, March 24, 1971, pp 2
[189] Janet Dolgin, <u>Jewish Identity and the JDL</u>, Princeton University Press, pp 37-38

Because of JDL's actions, the State and Justice Departments requested that Congress give them the Federal authority to prosecute cases involving attacks on American and foreign officials and the FBI assembled a comprehensive dossier on the Jewish Defense League beginning in the early 1970's. The government also used undercover agents to infiltrate and wiretapping surveillance in trying to undermine the JDL, on the orders of President Nixon on the grounds of national security.[190]

In October 1971, the League retaliated with a lawsuit charging the Justice Department with the use of an illegal wiretap and asking for a minimum of $732,800 in damages. The suit was a class action brought on behalf of all persons who made calls in and out of the JDL's office and former Attorney General John Mitchell and nine FBI agents were named as defendants.[191]

By the mid-1980's, the League had been labeled a "terrorist" organization by the FBI. None of this seemed to bother the JDL very much. Members continued to carry out their responsibilities, paying little heed to the plainclothesmen who kept an ominous eye on the League's offices. Realistically, law enforcement's response had minimal impact upon the main body of the League or its policies. In fact, in some cases, it served to bestow a hero's status upon those being prosecuted.

With members being arrested and sent to prison, the base of the pyramid began to erode and Kahane's shift of ideology to Aliyah caused internal opposition. "JDL'ers, not in full consciousness, masked the unique character of the Aliyah they were developing - particularly its proletarian origins - in stressing dramatic analogies between the situation of Jews in America and that in the Europe from which the early revisionists had come, and by stressing similarities between JDL and the revisionist movements at the expense of JDL's own specificity."[192]

---

[190] Eleanor Blau, <u>New York Times</u>, June 25, 1971, pp 23
[191] <u>New York Times</u>, October 8, 1971, pp 14
[192] Dolgin, Op.cit., pp 42

However, this was the paradox of the JDL's Aliyah ideology. How can you instigate a migration from a country where the majority of Jews feel comfortable and safe? How can you promote the Jewish nationalist trend if, on the other hand, you are trying to preserve the status quo of the urban Jew? This weakened the JDL's argument for Aliyah. "We feel that the Jew should get out of America while he can before he is forced out. We're hoping that we are wrong and we hope to show that we are wrong. That is why we are staying here," explained Marty Rosen. But, by placing defense before Aliyah, the JDL "has fallen into the same trap as the Jewish establishment, of trying to identify their interests with America's rulers' interests, rather than a true spirit of moral, cultural and political independence centered in Eretz Yisroel [land of Israel]."[193]

The Jewish Defense League drew its strength from the reality of its issues. It struck a nerve of undercurrent feeling in the grassroot Jew. Those who embraced assimilation have been strongly questioned and challenged by a surging nationalism. "For American Jews generally...JDL has shown that despite their rush to assimilate they still feel more Jewish than they did. It may have also shown them that they are a little less overwhelmingly, a little less unequivocally, opposed to violence than they once thought they were."[194] Yet, as early as 1971, Mel Ziegler expressed his opinion that the JDL would soon collapse because "legitimate and emotional" issues are scarce. The JDL "is due to feud itself to bits...once people get tired of hearing about Soviet Jewry."[195] Mr. Ziegler could not have been closer to the truth.

Kahane departed for Israel, eventually severing his ties with the JDL in 1985 to concentrate his efforts on domestic Israeli politics, creating a leadership void at the top of the pyramid. No one approached Kahane in terms of charisma, leadership,

---

[193] Mandel, Op.cit., pp 3
[194] Ziegler, Op.cit., pp 36
[195] Ibid. pp 36

influence or authority. It was his tight rein which helped to keep the group together despite heavy pressure to discredit it. Any laxity on those reins, coupled with an excess of power, will lead to internal splintering.

Such is the nature of a militant group demanding unquestioning loyalty and dedication from its members. Such a group cannot afford unchecked dissent. But with internal dissent comes a decline in membership and financial resources. "Kahane's prolonged absences from the U.S. have created a vacuum that over the years has nurtured the growth of competing bands of right-wing Jewish warlords, who are united only by the rabble-rousing rabbi's legacy of violence and Jewish machismo. It is a legacy that ...ultimately turned the JDL into a fratricidal movement, in which its members spend more time plotting against each other than against their gentile enemies."[196]

---

[196] Robert I. Friedman, "The Return of the JDL: Nice Jewish Boys with Bombs," Village Voice, May 6, 1986

Afterword

Rabbi Meir Kahane – madman, publicity-seeker, anarchist, criminal and terrorist. Or was he an activist, hero, brilliant political strategist and ahead of his time?   With the fiftieth anniversary of the founding of the Jewish Defense League in 2018, more than 45 years have passed since the majority of the research for this study was conducted. While the controversy continues regarding the impact that the JDL had, over time many elements within the American Jewish community have conceded that the JDL struck a chord that resonated with many American Jews.

It is clear from this examination of the early years of the JDL's existence that group conflict and political violence do play an influential role in affecting social change. "...By locking themselves in peaceful - or violent - conflict with some other element of society, social movements provoke trials of strength between contending forces or ideas...Through such trials...the agenda of controversy, the list of acceptable 'key' issues may be changed."[197]

What began in 1963 as a series of conversations between Herb Caron and Lou Rosenblum in their living rooms in suburban Cleveland, developed into a national grassroots awareness campaign to educate American Jewry about the plight of their brethren in the Soviet Union. In New York, British transplant Yakov Birnbaum was looking to find meaning to his life. Inspired by the enthusiasm of New York businessman Morris Brafman, he connected with Glenn Richter in 1964 and, together, they led student rallies to bring awareness of Soviet Jews seeking to emigrate to Israel. These groups plodded along for several years,

---

[197] Walker, Op. cit., pp 294

sometimes joining forces, but were stymied every step of the way by a "don't rock the boat" Jewish Establishment.

Only when the JDL stepped into the fray in 1969 did the issue of Soviet Jewry become front page news. That's when the trickle of emigrants became a small but steady flow. Soviet officials decided that the solution was to cut off the head of the snake by allowing the dissident leaders to leave for Israel. This strategy backfired because it encouraged others to renounce their Soviet citizenship and apply to emigrate. Throughout this period, the JDL kept up the pressure of harassment and disruption. In a June 1995 interview, Richter admitted that, "We could hold hundreds of peaceful demonstrations, but the fact was that it was the JDL that got the publicity."[198]

Ultimately, the destruction of the Berlin Wall in 1989 and the subsequent dissolution of the Soviet Union in 1991 led to the floodgates opening. During the 1990s, more than 1 million Soviet Jews left the former Soviet Union. More than 800,000 of them settled in Israel.

Even today, the Jewish Defense League stands out as a 20th century model for the successful use of group conflict and political violence. Other social movements, such as the Pro-Life/Anti-Abortion movement, have taken a similar path to achieving their political goals. No longer is political violence seen as a "last resort."

While the Jewish Defense League certainly played an important, militant role for the nationalist movement, as an issue-oriented group that relied heavily upon its militancy, it faced a limited life-span. The FBI began to crack down, labeling the JDL a terrorist group. Kahane was assassinated in 1990 and without Kahane, the JDL became splintered and eventually faded into obscurity by the year 2000 with its leadership rotting in jail.

---

[198] Walter Ruby, Op. cit. pp 208

The unfortunate truth is that as long as there are Jews, there will be Jew-haters. Anti-Semitism, while often subtle, can rear its ugly head from time to time, reminding us of what the JDL stood for. Well into the 21st century, Jews in America and around the world are still being attacked and murdered, right in their own homes, synagogues and businesses. Even today, white supremacists are often emboldened by political leaders who claim that "there are fine people" on both sides of the issue.

What is undeniable, however, is that the JDL, particularly during its early years, made points which were difficult to refute. Jews are afraid; there is anti-Semitism; there are Jews living in poverty; and the American Jewish community doesn't always respond adequately or with a sense of urgency. "But," asserted Richard Yaffee, chairman of the National Council of Americans for Progressive Israel-Hashomer Hatzair, "the answers do not lie at the end of a billy club or bicycle chain."[199]

Or do they, Mr. Yaffee? Can you promise us, "Never Again?"

---

[199] <u>Jewish Telegraphic Agency</u>, March 3, 1972, pp 4

Bibliography

<u>Books</u>

Appelbaum, Richard. Theories of Social Change, Chicago: Markham Publishing Company, 1970

Arendt, Hannah. On Violence, New York: Harcourt, Brace & World, Inc., 1970

Beckerman, Gal. When They Come For Us, We'll Be Gone, New York: Houghton Mifflin Harcourt, 2010

Coser, Lewis. The Functions of Social Conflict, New York: The Free Press, 1956

Dolgin, Janet. Jewish Identity and the JDL, New Jersey: Princeton University Press, 1977

Friedman, Murray and Albert D. Chernin, editors. A Second Exodus, The American Movement To Free Soviet Jews, Hanover, NH, Brandeis University Press, University Press of New England, 1999

Greeley, Andrew M. Why Can't They Be Like Us?, New York: American Jewish Committee, 1969

Gurr, Ted Robert. Why Men Rebel, Princeton, New Jersey: Princeton University Press, 1970

Kahane, Meir. Never Again, Los Angeles: Nash Publishing Corporation, 1971

Kahane, Meir. The Story of the Jewish Defense League, Radnor, Pennsylvania: The Chilton Book Company, first edition 1975

Lasswell, Harold. Politics: Who Gets What, When, How, Cleveland: Meridian Books, The World Publishing Company, 11th printing 1968; McGraw Hill Book Company, 1st printing 1936

Levin, Nora. Jews in the Soviet Union Since 1917: Paradox in Survival, New York: New York University Press, 1988

Lewin, Kurt. "When Facing Danger" 1939 and "Self-Hatred
    Among Jews" 1941 in Resolving Social Conflicts, ed.
    Gertrud W. Lewin, selected papers on group dynamics,
    New York: Harper & Row, Publishers, 1948

Nieburg, H. L. Political Violence: The Behavioral Process, New
    York: St. Martin's Press, 1970

Sorel, Georges. Reflections on Violence, translated by T. E. Hulme,
    London: Collier Books, Collier-MacMillan LTD, 4th
    printing, 1970; first printed in 1908

Tilly, Charles. "Collective Violence in European Perspective"
    Violence in America, ed. Hugh Graham and Ted Gurr,
    Washington, D.C.: U.S. Government Printing Office, 1969.
    A staff report to the National Commission of the Causes
    and Prevention of Violence

Journals

Chanes, Jerome A.   "Blacks and Jews in America: History, Myths,
    and Realities," Jerusalem Center For Public Affairs, March
    15, 2006

Mack, Raymond W. and Synder, Richard C. "The Analysis of Social
    Conflict-Toward an Overview and Synthesis," Bobbs &
    Merrill Reprint #PS-177, originally appeared in Conflict
    Resolution, Vol. 1, No. 2, June 1957, pp 212-248, Sage
    Publications, Inc.

Montalbano, Michael D.   Guide to the Records of National Jewish
    Community Relations Advisory Council 1940-1994,
    American Jewish Historical Society, 2002

Walker, Jack L. "A Critique of the Elitist Theory of Democracy,"
    The American Political Science Review, Vol. LX, No. 2,
    June 1966, pp 285-295

Wedge, Bryant. "The Case Study of Student Political Violence:
    Brazil 1964 and the Dominican Republic, 1965," World
    Politics, Vol. XXI (Jan. 1969) pp 195-196

Wertheimer, Jack. "Jewish Organizational Life in the U.S. Since
    1945," American Jewish Yearbook 1995, Vol. 95, pp 3 -98,
    Editor: David Singer; Executive Editor: Ruth R. Seldin,
    American Jewish Committee, New York

Magazines

Bongartz, Roy. "2. Superjew," Esquire Magazine, August 1970, pp
        110, 126-128
Flame, interview with Meir Kahane, "Jewish Is Beautiful," Vol. 5,
        No. 1, March 1971, pp 6-7
Goodman, Walter. "Rabbi Kahane says: 'I'd Love to See the J.D.L.
        Fold Up. But - '" New York Times Magazine, November
        21, 1971, pp 32
Klein Halevi, Yossie. "Glory," written November 25, 2010,
        appearing in New Republic, December 2, 2010
Lowenthal, Zvi and Braun, Jonathan. "Right on Judaism…JDL's
        Meir Kahane Speaks Out-An Interview," Flame, Vol 5, No.
        1, March 1971
Newsweek. "Brussels Conference" March 8, 1971, pp 72-73
Newsweek. "Diplomacy: Bully Tactics" January 18, 1971, pp 34
Peterson, John. "J.D.L. - Camp Builds Cadre of Street Fighters"
        National Observer, July 28, 1969, no page number
        available
Time. "Foreign Relations: Curbing the J.D.L." May 24, 1971, pp 21
Ziegler, Mel. "The Jewish Defense League and It's Invisible
        Constituency," New York Magazine, April 19, 1971, pp 28-
        36

Newspapers

Andelman, David. New York Times, May 13, 1971, pp 1, 15
Arnold, Martin. New York Times, April 23, 1971, pp 41
Blau, Eleanor. New York Times, May 25, 1971, pp23; July 7, 1971,
        pp75; July 10, 1971, pp 1, 24
Brady, Thomas. New York Times, May 23, 1970, p 1
Carmody, Deirdre. New York Times, March 31, 1971, pp 50
Fiske, Edward. New York Times, May 10, 1969, pp 32; May 21,
        1970, pp 14
Fox, Sylvan. New York Times, August 7, 1969, pp 25
Fraser, C. Gerald. New York Times, June 24, 1970, pp 14
Friedman, Robert I. "The Return of the JDL: Nice Jewish Boys with
        Bombs," Village Voice, May 6, 1986

Gansberg, Martin. New York Times, June 30, 1970, pp 45

Giniger, Henry. New York Times, February 25, 1971, pp 18

Haberman, Clyde. New York Times, January 27, 1972, pp 41

Haff, Joseph. New York Times, May 5, 1971. pp 34

Halloran, Richard. New York Times, January 9, 1971, pp 1

Hamill, Peter. "Beyond Reason," New York Post, January 27, 1972

Henehan, Donal. New York Times, February 2, 1970, pp 30

Jewish Liberation Journal, "Youth Occupy Federation," New York
        Federation Allocation Budget for 1968-1969, April-May
        1970, No. 7, pp 4-5

Jewish Week, Editorial, May 6, 1972, pp 1, article on pp 2

Jewish Week, Editorial, "Are the hotheads seizing control of the
        JDL?" May 20, 1971

Johnson, Rudy. New York Times, January 20, 1969, pp 22

Kaplan, Morris. New York Times, May 14, 1971, pp 1, 66; July 24,
        1971, pp 26; November 19, 1971, pp 54

Kaufman, Michael. New York Times, January 24, 1971, pp 1

Knight, Michael. New York Times, October 7, 1970, pp 1, 9

Kovac, Bill. New York Times, October 23, 1969, pp 1, 32

Lissner, Will. New York Times, January 21, 1971, pp 29

Lubasch, Arnold. New York Times, February 17, 1969, pp 68

New York Times, September 7, 1968, pp 1; September 9, 1968, pp
        1; September 10, 1968, pp 1; September 11, 1968, pp 1;
        September 12, 1968, pp 1; September 25, 1968, pp30;
        October 1, 1968, pp 1; October 2, 1968, pp 1; October 14,
        1968, pp 1; November 10, 1968, pp 85; January 27, 1969,
        pp 28; March 17, 1969, pp 31; May 18, 1969, pp 81;
        September 21, 1969, pp 6; October 8, 1969, pp 37;
        December 24, 1969, pp 3; December 26, 1969, pp 18;
        December 31, 1969, pp 18; January 1, 1970, pp 14;
        February 24, 1970, pp 12; June 4, 1970, pp 6; June 29,
        1970, pp 33; June 30, 1970, pp 45; July 28, 1970, pp 6;
        August 30, 1970, pp 9; October 12, 1970, pp 23; October
        13, 1970, pp 35;   November 13, 1970, pp 46;
        November 26, 1970, pp 48; December 14, 1970, pp 53;
        December 28, 1970, pp 3; January 11, 1971, pp 1; January
        16, 1971, pp 11;February 4, 1971, pp 70; February 15,
        1971, pp 11; February 18, 1971, pp 24; February 23, 1971,

pp 3; February 26, 1971, pp 2; March 22, 1971, pp 1; April
21, 1971, pp 5; May 1, 1971, pp 22; May 15, 1971, pp 30;
May 25, 1971, pp 22; May 27, 1971, pp 45; June 11, 1971,
pp 32; June 22, 1971, pp 22; July 26, 1971, pp 57;August
9, 1971, pp 4; August 10, 1971, pp 20; October 8, 1971,
pp 14;

Perlmutter, Emanuel. New York Times, June 25, 1970, pp 20; July
13, 1971, pp 11; August 25, 1971, pp 18; and August 31,
1971, pp 11

Phillips, McCandish. New York Times, June 25, 1969, pp 25

Schumach, Murray. New York Times, January 15, 1971, pp 8

Smith, Hedrick. New York Times, November 26, 1970, pp 1, 48

Spiegel, Irving. New York Times, May 19, 1969, pp 33; June 2,
1969, pp 88; October 10, 1969, pp 52; December 30,
1969, pp 1; May 25, 1970, pp 4; January 9, 1971, pp 1;
January 30, 1971, pp 34; and May 3, 1971, pp 26

Tomasson, Robert. New York Times, June 28, 1971, pp 18

Van Gelder, Lawrence. New York Times, December 12, 1970, pp
12; January 13, 1971, pp 15

Jewish Student Newspapers

Gurner, Steven. "The JDL: The Philosophy of the New Jew," Kol
Bo, published by the Chicago Jewish Student Press,
February 16, 1971, pp 4-5

Kaplan, Earl. "Visitor's Day at Camp," Kadima, published by the
independent college students of Illinois, Dec.-Jan. 1972,
pp 7-8

Kahane, Meir. "Jewish Is Beautiful" OR, published by the Jewish
students of York University, February 1971, Vol. 1, No. 6,
pp 1, 7

Polansky, Joe. "Little Big Jew," OR, published by the Jewish
students of York University, February 1971, Vol. 1, No. 6,
pp 8

Ratner, Robert. "Israel or Death," Te'chiyat Hanefesh, published
by the Jewish students of New York University, November
29, 1971, Vol. II, No. 3, pp 2

Bibliography 97

Schwartz, Bill. "Notes on A Demagogue," Hamagshimim Newsletter, a publication of Young Judaea, Inc., Vol. III, No. 3, January 1972, pp 11

Sperling Dov. "A Russian Jew Speaks," OR, published by the Jewish students of York University, February 1971, Vol. 1, No. 6, pp 6

Stanislawski, Michael. "Book Review - Kahane: Saving the Jews to Find Peace With Himself," Genesis2, published by the independent students of Boston, February 17, 1972, pp 9

Starr, Stuart. "A Critical Look at the JDL," Kol Bo, published by the Chicago Jewish Student Press, February 16, 1971, pp 4-5

Student Newsletters

Student Nonviolent Coordinating Committee Newsletter, THIRD WORLD ROUND UP, The Palestine Problem: Test Your Knowledge, June-July 1967, pp 4-5

Student Nonviolent Coordinating Committee, The Middle-East Crisis, August 15, 1967, pp 1-2

News Services

Goldberg, Leslie. "Community Seeks to Oust Nazis," Jewish Telegraphic Agency, (JTA), January 26, 1972, pp 1

Goldman, Robert. "World Jewish Leadership and Soviet Jewry," Jewish Student Press Service, 1972

Jewish Telegraphic Agency. October 14, 1968 pp 4; August 9, 1969; January 16, 1972, pp 1; March 3, 1972, pp 4; March 24, 1972, pp 3; January 27, 1972, pp 3; January 6, 1972, pp 3

Mandel, David. "A Radical Zionist's Critique of JDL," Jewish Student Press Service, 1971

"New York Board of Rabbis Harassed By JDL," Jewish Student Press Service, 1971

Internet

JewishVirtualLibrary.org
Prager, Dennis. Jewish Journal.com, August 8, 2012

Organizational Reports

"Fact Sheet - Jewish Defense League," published by the American
     Jewish Committee, prepared by the Trends Analyses
     Division, February 1970, updated January 1971
Anti-Defamation League. "ADL Press Survey: The JDL," February
     1971. ADL Memorandum recording a conversation
     between David Frost and Foreign Minister of Israel Abba
     Eban, condemning the JDL, October 20, 1971. "Is The JDL
     Bad for Jews?" a newsletter issued by the ADL
Facts, "The Jewish Defense League: Exploiter of Fear," February
     1971, Vol. 20, No. 1, published by the ADL

Jewish Defense League Literature

"Every Jew a .22"
JDL advertisement, New York Times, October 20, 1969, pp 52
"J.D.L. and You"
"Jews - go Home: The Case for Aliyah"
Shoshan, Shmuel. "Jew...Go Home"
"The Three Most Asked Questions of the JDL"

Interviews by the Author

Interviews for this book were conducted by the author with the
     following JDL members: Stuart Cohen, Sheldon Davis,
     Robert Fine, Marty Rosen and Morris Schwartz during the
     months of February and March 1972. Author also
     attended the speech given by John T. Hatchett at New
     York University.

Index

A

B

C